Syria under Bashar al-Asad: Modernisation and the Limits of Change

Volker Perthes

ADELPHI PAPER 366

Oxford University Press, Great Clarendon Street, Oxford OX2 6DP
Oxford New York

Athens Auckland Bangkok Bombay Calcutta Cape Town
Dar es Salaam Delhi Florence Hong Kong Istanbul Karachi
Kuala Lumpur Madras Madrid Melbourne Mexico City Nairobi
Paris Taipei Tokyo Toronto
and associated companies in Ibadan

Oxford is a trade mark of Oxford University Press

Published in the United States
by Oxford University Press Inc., New York

© The International Institute for Strategic Studies 2004

First published July 2004 by **Oxford University Press** for
The International Institute for Strategic Studies
Arundel House, 13–15 Arundel Street, Temple Place, London WC2R 3DX
www.iiss.org

Director John Chipman
Editor Tim Huxley
Manager for Editorial Services James Green
Copy Editor Matthew Foley
Production Simon Nevitt

British Library Cataloguing in Publication Data
Data available

Library of Congress Cataloguing in Publication Data

ISBN 0-19-856750-2
ISSN 0567-932x

Contents

Introduction

Syria in a Period of Change

Halfway through Bashar al-Asad's seven-year term as president of Syria, the country is still in transition. Bashar al-Asad assumed the presidency in July 2000, one month after the death of his father and predecessor Hafiz al-Asad, who had ruled the country since November 1970. Transition for Syria is multi-dimensional. The country inhabits a rapidly changing regional environment, and is undergoing a process of economic change which, in the long run, may add up to a full transformation from statism to a market economy. Certainly, Syria's new leaders have taken economics more seriously than their predecessors, and have prioritised it over political reform. There are few signs that the transition from the regime of Hafiz al-Asad to that of his son will imply the dismantling of the former's authoritarian structures. Externally, the first three years of Bashar al-Asad's tenure were marked by the breakdown of the Middle East peace process, by the Iraq war, and by its regional repercussions.

To foreign political observers, Syria has been of interest mainly because of its position in the Arab-Israeli conflict and peace process. Israel and Arab-Israeli issues have been the central foreign-policy concern of Syrian policymakers since at least 1967. This is hardly surprising, given that Syria and Israel have been at war with each other in 1948, 1967, 1973 and 1982, and have confronted each other in Lebanon, directly or by proxy, almost continuously for the last quarter of a century. While Syria's overarching concern with Israel is not in dispute, there are different theoretical assumptions about what essentially guides its behaviour in the conflict, and its foreign policy in general. Patrick Seale, a veteran observer of Syria, emphasises regional power politics, or the struggle for regional predominance.[1]

Moshe Ma'oz stresses Syria's interest in finding an acceptable settlement with Israel.[2] Less convincing are approaches that see ideological motives[3] or sectarian bonds as the main driving force behind Syria's policies in the region.[4] Under Hafiz al-Asad, Syria had been much too pragmatic, and its foreign policy fitted more easily into a realist framework of analysis, whereby states try to pursue their national interests in mostly dangerous regional or international environments.[5] Beyond this, there has always been a politico-economic dimension to Syria's regional relations: trade relations, labour migration and financial support from other states have all depended on Syria's position and policies in the region.[6]

No one expected the succession from Hafiz to Bashar al-Asad to initiate a radical break with the past. Neither domestic- nor foreign-policy directions shifted abruptly. Rather, a new leadership structure has emerged. While strengthening their position, Asad and his team had to react both to structural needs and to events, thereby developing and adapting an agenda that was not fundamentally opposed to their predecessors', but was in many respects distinguishable from it.

What, then, moves Syria? This study highlights three main factors. The first is the resource factor: Syria, whatever the regime, needs to secure the resources to meet growing societal demands, as well as to maintain a political system that is still built, to some extent at least, on the capacity of its leaders to distribute privilege. Second, there is the generational factor: not only is the leadership generation that has been in charge for almost three decades being replaced relatively quickly, but political actors also tend to explain struggles and conflicts over policy issues in part in generational terms. The third factor is changing regional geopolitics. Syria is an active player in the Middle East, but it is not in control of regional events. Relations with its neighbourhood tend to have a strong impact on domestic developments. Syria's leaders may not always act wisely, but they have rational and legitimate security concerns. Syria, after all, finds itself in a rough environment, and one likely to remain so for some years to come.

Chapter 1

Managing Modernisation: Domestic Politics and the Limits of Change

When Hafiz al-Asad, Syria's president for almost three decades, died in June 2000, the question of succession was already settled. Nonetheless, the way state and party institutions handled the change was still impressive: within hours of the announcement of Asad's death, Syria's parliament or People's Council (*majlis al-sha'b*) had changed the constitution, lowering the minimum age required for the presidency from 40 to 34, thereby allowing Bashar al-Asad, the president's son, to stand for the job. Within two weeks, the Ba'ath party and the parliament had made the younger Asad the official and only candidate for the presidency. Within less than six weeks, a referendum had been held, Bashar al-Asad had duly been elected with an official 97.3% result, and had been sworn in.[1]

With this quasi-monarchical succession, Bashar al-Asad assumed the leadership of a highly centralised, authoritarian presidential system shaped during his father's rule. He also moved into all of the latter's formal positions: even before his election as president, he was made commander-in-chief of the Syrian army and general-secretary of the Ba'ath party. As the president, he also heads the Progressive National Front, mostly referred to simply as the Front (*al-jabha*), a formal alliance that joins a number of smaller tolerated parties with the 'leading' Ba'ath party. He appoints and dismisses the cabinet, judges, provincial governors, university presidents and other senior officials; he can dissolve parliament, parliamentary decisions need his consent to become law, and he has legislative powers of his own. All formal chains of command thus come together at the president's office.

When taking office, Bashar al-Asad made it clear that his immediate priorities lay in the domestic rather than the foreign-policy field. Hafiz al-Asad had spent most of his time and energy on regional politics, not least the Arab-Israeli conflict and the peace process. Syria's course in this field was not in dispute; the young president promised continuity and reconfirmed that peace was the country's 'strategic choice'. However, contrary to his predecessor, he would pay more attention to Syria's developmental 'performance'. Bashar al-Asad spoke extensively of the need to reform, improve and modernise the economy, education and administration. He also raised expectations of political change by emphasising 'democratic thinking' and 'the principle of accepting the opinion of the other'.[2]

As the succession process had come about more smoothly than many had expected, Syrian and foreign observers began to ask whether Bashar al-Asad would manage to consolidate power; whether he would be willing and able to change domestic political structures; and whether he would set the country on the path of economic reform and recovery. The three tasks were clearly interrelated.

Changing generations

Bashar al-Asad owed his position to the regime at the top of which he had been placed. At the outset, therefore, it seemed that some sort of collective leadership would emerge, whereby the president would have to share power with other members of the leadership, particularly those who had been brought into their posts by his father. Three years into his tenure, Bashar al-Asad is still not the source of all power, as his father had been, but he has become the prime decision-maker. Occasionally, he has had to compromise over policy issues and personnel decisions. When a new cabinet was formed in 2003, the party leadership blocked the appointment of some more reform-minded candidates on the prime minister's list – and the president chose not to support these candidates. Some of Hafiz al-Asad's influential barons still play an important role, but they do not constitute a threat to the president's position. These barons are usually referred to as the 'old guard' – a concept that oversimplifies when used not only to describe the composition of Syria's political élite, but also to explain political processes.

Bashar al-Asad's power derives from various sources. First, of course, he is the president. Within the party, as well as within the

Alawi sect to which his family and most security chiefs belong, he enjoys legitimacy as his father's heir. Beyond this circle, he is regarded as representative of the younger generation in a regime that had become gerontocratic during his father's long tenure. He also possesses the advantage of knowledge vis-à-vis those representing the old regime élite. After the death of his older brother in 1994, Bashar al-Asad built an image for himself as a counsel to his father and a succession candidate who knew what globalisation and new technologies were about. In contrast to most members of the regime élite, Bashar al-Asad could claim to be up to date with the world. Furthermore, and again in contrast to most of the old regime, he enjoys some popularity.

Finally, Bashar al-Asad has consolidated his power by systematically appointing trusted people to important positions. The transition was thus accompanied by a wide-ranging change in leadership personnel: within less than two years, three-quarters of the 60 or so top political, administrative and military office-holders had been replaced. Within the first weeks of the new era, all editors-in-chief of the state-run media were removed. In the following months, practically all provincial governors and provincial heads of the Ba'ath were replaced. In 2002, elections to lower-level party leaderships brought about significant changes among functionaries. In 2003, a new parliament was voted in. While its political colouring did not change – the Ba'ath party's majority had been officially fixed beforehand – the turnover was impressive: 178 of the chamber's 250 members were newcomers.

No comparably wide-ranging change in membership of the political élite had occurred since Hafiz al-Asad's takeover 30 years earlier.[3] Although Bashar al-Asad continues to rely on some advisors inherited from his father – among them Foreign Minister Faruq al-Sharaa, who has held that office since 1984 – a new generation took over on almost all levels. From the president's perspective, such a thorough renewal and rejuvenation of the political and administrative élite was necessary not only to gather support for his ideas about reform, but also to increase, albeit gradually, the number and weight of people within the institutions of power who owed their position, and thus their loyalty, to him - not to his father or to the old regime.

Bashar al-Asad's personal choices and priorities seem to be best represented in the cabinet, particularly with regard to portfolios dealing with economic policy issues, technology, training and education. Most of these ministers are technocrats oriented towards technical modernisation and integration into the world economy. Most hold university degrees from Western countries, often in engineering or economics. Several members of what can be called Asad's reform team are 'independents': they do not belong to the Ba'ath or any of the Front parties; several are leading members of the Syrian Computer Society (SCS). Bashar al-Asad presided over the SCS until his ascent to the presidency. This was the only official position he held at that time, and it helped him to build his image as a moderniser.

Rejuvenation was not restricted to political appointees. In March 2002, the government decreed that all civil servants over the age of 60 would be retired. The decision, which affected some 80,000 employees, allowed younger cadres to be promoted, and offered opportunities for new entrants. Some exceptions to forced retirement proved necessary, particularly in the foreign ministry, where diplomats with ample experience were scarce, and in the security apparatus. The regulation allowed the current leadership generation to quickly gain dominance over the civil service.

This wide-ranging renewal of state and party personnel clearly includes neo-patrimonial aspects, in that it enables the president to build his own network of loyalists. Nonetheless, most new appointees represent better and more effective governance. These newcomers also have a more discursive and transparent style than their predecessors, particularly in dealing with the public. Ministers now give press conferences, or respond to critical questions at public gatherings. Most of those appointed to relevant state or party positions under Bashar al-Asad are also regarded as relatively 'clean'. While the same did not apply to many of those the president inherited from his father's team and to some members of his own wider family, recruitment policies have certainly heeded Asad's proclaimed commitment to fighting corruption. Political loyalty or active membership in the Ba'ath party are no longer sufficient to enable a move into senior administrative positions. The Ba'ath party itself has made an effort to raise the formal qualifications of its functionaries: for the 2003 parliamentary elections, Ba'athist candidates standing in the 'peasant and worker' category – for which half of seats are reserved – were required to hold a high-school certificate, and all other candidates at least a bachelor's degree.[4]

Many low- or mid-level party cadres in their thirties and forties tend to view the process of personnel change at the higher levels of the party and the state in generational terms, not in terms of political orientation. They emphasise that their generation is more modern, more technologically versed and more open to the world; they complain that, except for the president himself, the 'generation Bashar' is not represented in the highest political leadership, and they insist on the need to 'improve the quality' of state and party functionaries. This does not, however, indicate that the new generation necessarily has an alternative agenda to its predecessors or those it seeks to replace. Bashar al-Asad, in an interview with al-Arabiyah TV, was frank on this: if the 'old guard' were seeking to safeguard their interests, the 'new guard' might be those who 'want to join the group and do the same thing'. Many officials had been replaced, but the real issue was 'one of the general system'.[5] As a senior intelligence figure put it: 'Our main problem is not the old guard. It's the old structures'.[6]

Reforming the system or modernising authoritarianism?

Bashar al-Asad's accession to the presidency raised expectations that the era of authoritarianism in Syria would eventually come to an end. Whether because of his growing influence or because the regime felt more secure than it had in earlier periods, Syria's authoritarianism had become milder in the last years of Hafiz al-Asad's rule. But the structures that the elder Asad built to secure his regime were all still in place when Bashar took power.

Inherited structures

Syria never developed into a totalitarian or, as Alan George has it, an 'Orwellian' state.[7] Under Hafiz al-Asad, an authoritarian system and a strong security state emerged, supported by an often extreme personality cult, but this system did not try to build society according to one ideology, or enforce thought control over its subjects.[8] Hafiz al-Asad's regime was highly personalised; in a way, Syria became *Suriya al-Asad*, as so many banners or murals told the public. Asad's control over the system was partly achieved by 'neo-patrimonial' means, particularly the use of patronage networks built on family, tribal, confessional and regional ties.[9]

At the same time, an institutionalised form of authoritarianism came into being. This concentrated vast powers in the hands of the president, guaranteeing in practice that the president cannot be replaced by constitutional means unless he himself decides to leave office. The system rests on three main pillars: the centralised government bureaucracy, the Ba'ath party (officially *hizb al-Ba'ath al-'arabi al-ishtiraki*), and the security apparatus. The Ba'ath, one of the torch-bearers of pan-Arab nationalism from its establishment in the mid-1940s, has been the de facto regime party in Syria since 1963. Under Hafiz al-Asad, a handful of smaller Arab nationalist or leftist parties were readmitted to politics on the condition that they allied themselves with the Ba'ath and accepted its leadership within the Progressive National Front. The existence of the Front as well as the leading role of the Ba'ath within it was written into the constitution. Soon after Asad's takeover, the party was reorganised in a more hierarchic, centralised manner, and committed to supporting the leader; membership was inflated and the party effectively turned into an instrument of mobilisation and control. Corporatist elements, notably so-called 'popular' or mass organisations such as the General Federation of Trade Unions and the General Peasants Union, introduced an element of representation and enhanced the regime's ability to penetrate and control the active parts of society.

Ultimately, the power of the regime depends on the security apparatus, that is the army and the various intelligence or security services, generally referred to as the *mukhabarat*. The latter remain the main instrument of control, and certainly the most powerful agencies in the state. They are deeply involved in the day-to-day running of the country. Security clearances are needed for any public employment or promotion, and for social and, of course, political activity; even office or promotion within the Ba'ath party needs the prior agreement of the *fira' al-amn*, the relevant 'security' branch. The services maintain a vast network of informers, and can still arrest and hold people at will. While they often choose less repressive methods, they make their presence known, watching universities and public gatherings, screening relatives and neighbours and keeping under surveillance tolerated opposition groups and individual dissenters. Outside Damascus, the country is practically governed by the *mukhabarat*. This is done through so-called security committees, which consist of the provincial governor, the head of the party branch and the *mukhabarat* chief. While the latter's formal rank is lower than that of the others, his word is weightier. The national heads of the security agencies are considered to be within the innermost decision-making circle.[10]

Signs of openness

Bashar al-Asad's ascent to power set off widespread expectations of change. Bashar al-Asad himself nurtured such hopes and expectations, through his initial statements, through practical measures of high symbolic significance and through the introduction of fresh blood into the political and administrative élite.

The new president's inaugural speech in particular was widely regarded as a declaration of reform intentions.[11] Asad's talk of 'democratic thinking' and the 'principle of accepting the opinion of the other' lent itself favourably to a liberal interpretation. In substance, however, he did not commit himself to democratic reform, let alone a transformation of the political system to liberal democracy – speaking, rather, of the need to 'have our democratic experience which is special to us' and commending the Progressive National Front as a 'democratic example'.

Despite such vagueness, Syrian as well as foreign observers were impressed by the speech. It did, at least, reflect on domestic policy and structures, and it clearly emphasised the role of institutions, the need to respect the law, administrative reform and the fight against waste and corruption. Asad also laid out a series of steps that signalled a move towards greater political openness. Some had practical implications, others at least symbolic importance. Thus, an import ban on satellite receiver dishes – which had not been very effective anyway – was scrapped. Later in the year, the Mezze military prison outside Damascus, the temporary 'home' for generations of political opponents, was declared closed. Some 600 political prisoners of Islamist and leftist tendencies were given amnesty. A memorandum by 99 Syrian intellectuals published in the Lebanese press, calling on the authorities to scrap martial law, set free political prisoners and grant political freedoms, did not see any of the signatories arrested or harassed by the *mukhabarat*; some were even allowed to publish articles in the local, state-controlled press. The authorities let it be known that the president, while not particularly happy about being approached through foreign newspapers, did not, in principle, object to statements of citizen concerns. The release of the memorandum itself was a sign of change: it demonstrated that a public political debate had begun in Syria, and that – to use the oft-quoted term of Syrian writer Abd al-Razzaq Aid – the 'complex of fear' ('*uqdat al-khauf*) that had so long paralysed Syria's civil society had been broken. In stark contrast to the subdued and largely stagnant political atmosphere that had characterised most of Hafiz al-Asad's era, Syria found itself engaged in a broad political debate. This was neither totally open nor all-encompassing, but it involved voices and views that had hitherto been marginalised.

The political spectrum

Within the regime élite itself, three broad tendencies shaped the debate and affected political developments in the wake of Bashar al-Asad's rise to power.

The first tendency can be characterised as conservative. Its proponents want to maintain the political system and, to the extent possible, the domestic and foreign-policy course that Syria stood for under Hafiz al-Asad. Representatives of this tendency acknowledge that mistakes have occurred and 'corrections' have to be made, but their main message is that continuity is key: that the achievements of the old regime must not be ignored, and the system should be preserved. This applies to domestic 'stability', which would be threatened by too rapid steps towards political or economic liberalisation, as well as to Syria's Arab nationalist positions in regional and international questions, often referred to as 'fundamentals' (*thawabit*). Representatives of this trend include members of the old guard, such as Vice-President Abd al-Halim Khaddam, as well as some younger members of the élite. While it is difficult to gauge the support this tendency could muster, it has a social basis among the government, party and trade-union bureaucracy, and also among the intellectual bureaucracy, i.e. state-dependent writers, journalists or professors who owe their position to the system and to Ba'athist Arab nationalism.

Those in the second tendency can be referred to as modernisers. With Bashar al-Asad and his reform team at its core, this tendency represents the dominant trend. Its adherents are aware that structures and policies have to be reformed if Syria wants to survive in an increasingly competitive regional and international environment, and they see the need to renew or at least retrain cadres and leadership personnel. Otherwise, their emphasis is on technical modernisation and gradualism. Political change will eventually come about, but should build upon social and economic modernisation, rather than precede it, lest instability ensues. The social basis of this tendency includes not only the technocratic élite, but also large numbers of party newcomers, younger people within the Ba'ath who feel that their career chances have been blocked by the old generation. In addition, parts of the security establishment sense that continued stagnation and lack of technical adjustment may endanger the system as much as sudden change or political upheaval.

A third tendency is more critical of the entire system, and consequently emphasises the need for fundamental change. This diffuse and unorganised tendency can be referred to as democratic reformist. Generally, representatives of this trend have not cut their links to the state or to the government. Rather, they hope for a coalition of sorts with the modernisers. While most would still be prepared to cooperate with the president and his technocratic reformers, they ultimately seek a transformation of the system, and so find themselves in opposition to the regime as it is. Most hold that economic or administrative reform is no longer possible without political reforms, emphasising particularly the need to establish the rule of law and overcome the de facto one-party system. This tendency, which was substantially weakened through the arrests and subsequent trials of some of its leaders in 2001, has been represented by liberal intellectuals such as economics professor Aref Dalila, writer and journalist Michel Kilo, lawyer Anwar al-Bunni and other signatories of the 'Memorandum of the 99', as well as independent politicians such as Riad Seif, a prominent industrialist. It also includes a substantial number of former adherents to various nationalist or radical leftist groupings and even some, mainly younger, Ba'ath party members. Representatives of this tendency are not necessarily in contact or cooperating with each other: this is not an organisation of card-carrying members.

Spring (and Autumn) in Damascus

Various representatives of this democratic-reformist trend became the core of the so-called 'civil-society movement' that emerged within weeks of Bashar al-Asad's assumption of the presidency. While visible activities concentrated on Damascus, actors all over the country felt encouraged to make their voices heard and reinvigorate political life. There were differences over tactics, over the speed of action, or over the wording of declarations, but these should not, as Alan George points out, be exaggerated. Different actors were in fact 'engaged in separate but complementary projects';[13] the concurrence and plurality of activities made for a real movement that helped to change the political atmosphere. Activists and foreign observers – even some of the reformers around the president – began to speak of a 'Damascus Spring'.

In August 2000, the independent politician Riad Seif announced the establishment of an association of 'Friends of Civil Society'. Two weeks later, Seif established a forum in his home offering a series of public lectures on political issues. At about the same time, Syrian intellectuals began to publish open letters and opinion pieces on domestic policy issues in the Lebanese press, generally calling for political reform and liberties, and on 27 September the 'Memorandum of the 99' appeared. In the months that followed, parts of Syria's state-controlled media, particularly the daily *al-Thaura*, joined the debate about reform, and opened its pages to authors who were outspokenly critical of the regime. 'Political salons' like Seif's spread quickly.[14] Ba'thists, while trying to defend the party line, were clearly attracted by the atmosphere and content of the debate.

In January 2001, a new, more detailed statement prepared by the organisers of the 'Memorandum of the 99' was released, or rather leaked to the press. This so-called 'Basic Document of the Committees for the Revival of Civil Society' repeated the main demands of the first memorandum, but added a sharp critique of the Ba'athist era, particularly the way in which it had done away with earlier democratic and constitutional achievements. Without mentioning the party by name, it refuted the Ba'athist claim to lead the state and society on the basis of 'revolutionary legitimacy', demanded a democratic election law and freedom of organisation, and called for the country-wide establishment of committees for the revival of civil society. Also in January, some 20 deputies formed what they called an 'Independent Parliamentary Bloc', and 70 lawyers published a statement demanding an end to the state of emergency in place since 1963, the independence of the judiciary and the legalisation of political parties. By this stage, half a year after the presidential succession, the democratic-reformist trend had clearly become a political factor that could not be ignored. Although it did not constitute a mass movement, it contributed substantially to the political discourse.

For the conservatives within the regime élite, such developments were anathema. The president himself seemed to be increasingly annoyed by the criticisms being made by the civil-society movement; he had clearly no interest in being harried into deeper and more rapid changes than he and his team deemed necessary or advisable. The regime leadership therefore went on a counter-offensive. Initially trying to win back dominance in the political debate, they soon reverted to administrative and, eventually, repressive methods. Thus, in February, members of the party leadership went on lecture and debate tours to reassure party cadres in the provinces and the universities. Khaddam, for example, warned university professors that intellectuals were spreading ideas that threatened national unity. Was it the Algerian example, he asked, the breakup of order and the civil war that followed Algeria's political opening, that the intellectuals wanted to copy?[16] Several officials spoke of 'red lines' which the intellectuals had overstepped. Asad himself, in an interview with the Saudi newspaper *al-Sharq al-Awsat*, declared that it was only natural to ignore statements of intellectuals that were spread through channels outside the country. It seemed, Asad continued, that those who released such memoranda 'prefer the stages of coups and occupation to the stability that started in 1963 and was enhanced in 1970' – since his father's coup, that is. In March, Asad made it clear that national unity, the Ba'ath party, the armed forces and the 'path of the late leader Hafiz al-Asad' were not open for discussion.[18] Other representatives of the regime accused the intellectuals of being 'hateful', ignoring the Arab-Israeli struggle and denigrating the achievements of the Ba'athist era. Defence Minister Mustafa Tlass warned that 'we will not accept that anybody take the power from us, because it comes from the barrel of the gun, and we are its masters'.[19]

Although an authoritarian response to the civil-society movement was obviously being prepared, not everybody in the regime or in the vicinity of the president wanted to do away with the new climate of openness. In mid-February, the authorities put a stop to most of the salons by imposing administrative requirements that were virtually impossible for them to meet. Individual activists were warned not to continue their activities. Seif's parliamentary immunity was lifted to allow for criminal investigations on a charge of having violated the constitution. Articles denouncing Seif as a puppet in foreign hands were launched in a populist pro-regime magazine published in Lebanon, and in a private 'satirical' magazine.[20] At the same time, however, Mahmud Salamah, the editor-in-chief of the government newspaper *al-Thaura*, wrote an editorial in which he asserted that the 'Damascus Spring' was just about to start: 'National consensus cannot be achieved in a society of parrots or by means of unilateral official discourse. It is achieved through political, economic and cultural pluralism'.[21] Salamah came under increasing pressure from the minister of information, who eventually dismissed him in May.

The dismissal of Salamah – who had been put into his position by Bashar al-Asad – was a clear sign that the president had allied himself with the regime conservatives. Increasingly, Syria's media replaced the term 'reform and renewal' (al-islah wa-l-tajdid), which had been used to denote the new era, with 'development and modernisation' (*al-tatwir wa-l-tahdith*). This changing atmosphere also reflected on the civil-society movement. Groups and individuals who had set up salons kept a low profile. The group of intellectuals that had launched the two previous memoranda released another statement. This upheld basic demands for democracy and the rule of law, but it also sought to appease the regime by introducing some of its nationalist discourse, speaking not only of Arab unity, but also of the 'racist Israeli Zionist enemy'. However, democracy was the 'necessary entry-point and the sharpest weapon to win this battle'.[22]

Those who stuck to signing such statements were not molested. Others were. In August, Ma'mun Homsi, an independent deputy who had begun to publicly attack the intelligence apparatus, was arrested. In September, Seif resumed the activities of his salon by inviting expatriate Syrian sociologist Burhan Ghalioun to speak. Within days, Seif and eight of his friends, among them economist Arif Dalila who had a long record of speaking out against corruption and mismanagement, were arrested. Riad al-Turk, a veteran communist leader who had spent 17 years in prison under Hafiz al-Asad, was also seized after he called the late president a 'dictator' on the al-Jazeera satellite channel. All were subsequently put on trial. Seif and Homsi were sentenced to five-year prison terms, Arif Dalila to ten years and the others to between two and five years.[23] The arrests dealt a severe blow to the liberal-democratic trend and disappointed many who had pinned their hopes for political change on the president. The regime had drawn a line, and the security agencies had asserted their dominance in matters of domestic politics. Nonetheless, the political debate continued, albeit privately rather than in public or semi-public spaces. Even the civil-society 'Committees' continued to meet and to voice their opinions through the Lebanese press, the international media and the internet. But the Damascus Spring was clearly over.

Asad's agenda

Bashar al-Asad may have decided to attack the democratic reformist trend in order to strengthen his own position within the regime. He may also simply have become increasingly annoyed by demands for speedier change, and by the accusations of incompetence and corruption levelled against his regime by individual deputies and intellectuals. It is less likely that he or his team actually believed the regime's propaganda depicting Seif and his friends as 'foreign agents'. Such allegations travelled well with the more simple-minded elements of the regime's political base, but were rarely heard from members of the regime élite once Seif and his colleagues were imprisoned. Nor were the official charges on which the dissidents were tried taken seriously.[24]

Some regime officials sought to legitimise the crackdown on the civil-society movement by claiming that these activists had done the wrong thing at the wrong time, with insufficient consideration of Syria's geopolitical situation. As a member of Asad's reform team put it, how could the president allow himself to be pressured by a couple of intellectuals while Sharon was at the gates?[25] Although regional tension might not, in the end, have been the motive for the regime's repressive moves, the intensification of the Arab–Israeli and particularly the Israeli–Palestinian conflict from September 2000, and the election of Ariel Sharon as Israel's prime minister in February 2001, clearly made it easier for the modernisers around the president to accept the arguments of, and close ranks with, the more conservative elements within the party leadership and security apparatus.

Beyond that, Bashar al-Asad's own agenda, and that of most of the young regime élite, is one of modernisation, not systemic change or democratisation. Asad has left little doubt about his priorities: they are in the domestic-policy field, but they pertain to economic development and administrative reform in the widest sense. The issue was 'not ... to undermine, but to develop the reality'.[26] The idea, in other words, was to modernise the authoritarian system, not to dismantle it. Members of the president's reform team are not inimical to liberal democracy as a concept, and certainly not to democracy in Europe or America. As far as Syria is concerned, however, they tend to build on elements of classic modernisation theory: the demand for democracy in a Western sense, they argue, is premature as long as people are poor and lack education. Society was not ripe yet, but would become so, gradually, in line with the progress of Bashar al-Asad's modernisation project.

Developing political institutions

Three years into the presidential succession, many Syrians complain that nothing has changed, that the regime is still as it was. At the same time, members of the regime élite claim that the system has actually been developing. This claim is not unfounded. The élite has in fact embarked on what could be called a gradualistic and authoritarian modernisation project – but one that falls short of the wishes and expectations of domestic liberals and many of Syria's foreign partners. Its main thrust has been to raise the efficiency of the state and the economic system. Aside from changing much of the personnel, or rejuvenating the political and administrative élite through the co-option of younger and generally better-educated people, this project involves a limited range of political-structural aspects – namely a strongly-controlled form of pluralisation, and efforts to increase the weight of state institutions.

To start with, Syria's media landscape has become more pluralistic, and censorship milder. This reflects the sense of the younger generation in power that, in a world of satellite television and the internet, the traditional methods of control have become outdated. Satellite dishes became normal during the second part of the 1990s, and their import has been legalised. The pan-Arab *al-Hayat* and *al-Sharq al-Awsat* newspapers, as well as Lebanese, Jordanian or Gulf Arab titles, are regularly available. Since 2001, the Front parties have been issuing their own weekly newspapers, and a handful of privately owned magazines have been licensed. These include the satirical *al-Doumari*, the business-oriented *al-Iqtisadiyya*, the political news magazine *Abyad wa-Aswad* ('Black and White'), and a society magazine called *Layalina* ('Our Nights'), in which Syria's *jeunesse dorée* celebrates itself. Some of the Front party newspapers, such as *al-Iqtisadiyya* and *Abyad wa-Aswad*, have become outlets for liberal criticism, and for cautious demands for faster, deeper reform. However, this is not press freedom. Any periodical, even non-political advertising magazines, still needs a licence from the prime minister. Although *al-Doumari* toed the official political line on critical issues, it occasionally became subject to censorship, and was eventually closed down by the minister of information in 2003. The official reason for the closure was that the editors had refused to distribute their magazine through the official public-sector distributing agency which the ministry of information uses as an instrument of control. Journalists may also still find themselves behind bars, accused of spreading 'false news'.

In the realm of political representation, the regime leadership has evidently been torn between its unwillingness to allow for open political competition, and its realisation that the quasi one-party system is no longer sufficient to give all societal groups which the regime considers relevant a proper representation within the system. As far back as 1990, the regime of Hafiz al-Asad had responded to the need to integrate into the system hitherto unrepresented social actors whose economic, cultural or intellectual inputs were seen as necessary, by increasing the number of independent – non-Ba'ath or Front-party – deputies in parliament to around one-third of the 250 seats.[27] Most were businesspeople or tribal and religious leaders. Occasionally, individual representatives of officially unrecognised political groupings such as the Syrian Socialist Nationalist Party (SSNP)[28] and some Kurdish groups ran on an 'independent' ticket. In its official discourse, the regime began to speak of political pluralism.

Bashar al-Asad repeatedly commended the 'front' system, speaking of it as a home-grown example of democracy that would be 'developed'.[29] Consequently, there has been talk of expanding the Front by admitting other pro-regime groupings, among them the SSNP. Increasing the number of Front parties would not, however, make much of a difference. Except for one wing of the Syrian Communist Party (SCP), none of the nine Front parties constitutes a living political organisation. Some of them resemble family enterprises; their membership is largely ossified, and based on their rhetoric it is almost impossible to distinguish one from the other, or from the Ba'ath party.[30]

The regime has become more tolerant towards opposition groups that it does not consider a threat. This applies particularly to the so-called National Democratic Bloc, an alliance of parties of Nasserist, nationalist or leftist origin, such as the 'Communist Party Politbureau' under Riad Turk, and the Democratic Arab Socialist Union, a remnant of Gamal Abd al-Nasser's regime party, whose pro-regime breakaway wing forms part of the Front. These groups are able to meet, release press statements, maintain accessible websites and participate in public events. Some of their leaders command great respect even within regime circles. Inasmuch as these groups are grounded in the ideologies of the 1950s or 1960s and most of their leadership personnel hail from the generation of Hafiz al-Asad, they do not constitute a real challenge to the regime. In July 2003, the Democratic Arab Socialist Union received permission from the security agencies to hold a public celebration to mark Nasser's revolution of 1952.

In the case of the Islamist opposition, the regime's attitude is less relaxed. The Muslim Brotherhood, which led a bloody struggle against the regime in the late 1970s and early 1980s, is still banned. The Brotherhood has renounced violence; since Bashar al-Asad's accession, it has been developing a democratic discourse, and has reached out to liberals and leftists.[31] For the regime leadership, the prospect of cooperation between liberal-democratic and Islamist opposition forces is disturbing. While members of the Brotherhood have been released from prison or allowed to return from exile, there is no sign that the regime would consider legalising or tolerating Brotherhood activities. Under Hafiz al-Asad, unsuccessful attempts were made to find a credible figure prepared to form a party with an Islamist touch under the umbrella of the Front. The re-emergence of an Islamist party outside regime control, particularly if it had a deep social reach, would be unacceptable.

In a noticeable divergence from the old Ba'athist rhetoric, representatives of the regime have acknowledged that an opposition with legitimate positions and demands exists. 'There are no enemies of the regime,' Bahjat Sulaiman, one of Syria's security chiefs, wrote in a remarkable article in Lebanon's *al-Safir* in May 2003. 'There are 'opponents' of it; their opposition, however, does not drive them further than demanding the implementation of some political and economic reforms such as abolishing the state of emergency ... issuing a party law, and rationalising the distribution of national wealth.'[32] Here, Sulaiman's analysis is largely to the point - there are indeed no militant domestic enemies which the regime would have to fear, and opponents are quite prepared to cooperate with the government if their main political demands are met. Sulaiman's article also reveals the specific understanding of political plurality among the modernisers in the regime, namely that dissidents may speak their mind. At the same time, the regime élite has demonstrated that it will not allow such political forces to challenge its power.

This form of authoritarian pluralism allows for wider representation, but not for real competition. Consequently, the first parliamentary elections under Bashar al-Asad, in March 2003, followed the model of previous polls. Competition was restricted to the 83 slots reserved for independent candidates, while the results for two-thirds of the seats were predetermined. Known opposition figures refrained from standing or withdrew their candidature, and the turnout was low, according to both official and unofficial accounts.[33] Following these elections – and following, more importantly perhaps, the Iraq war – even some Ba'athist functionaries began to speak of the need for a party law that would allow groups outside the Front to stand for future elections. The regime élite, however, did not give the impression that it would agree to such a substantial change.

Administrative reform

For Asad, administrative reform has been the keyword from the beginning. Over-centralisation is a severe problem, and a main element of what Syrians refer to as *al-birukratiyya* – cumbersome, non-transparent, inefficient and often disdainful administrative behaviour and routine. There is little a civil servant below the rank of minister can decide. A small entrepreneur planning to open a restaurant in a provincial town would until recently have needed the approval of the minister of tourism. NGOs need ministerial permission to work, as well as security clearances; a private school has to acquire a presidential licence. A professor or any other senior civil servant who wants to be sent on an academic or business mission abroad needs the prime minister's approval. Decisions over television programmes or contributions to a newspaper that might be seen as critical may be referred to the minister of information, or even the president.

Syria's new political leadership has realised that such bureaucratic decision-making processes have to be streamlined, and that foreign expertise may be needed to do this. Accordingly, in 2003, a group of French consultants was brought in to plan and oversee the restructuring of an initial group of ministries. Bad administrative practice is of course not only a technical problem, but ultimately one of governance. Not only does *al-birukratiyya* multiply the opportunities for bribery and extortion, it adds to the difficulty of overcoming it. Syria's administrative cadres, due to a deep-rooted authoritarian culture grown over some 40 years, generally lack the capacity and preparedness to take decisions. State employees have learned that individual initiatives and decisions may be risky, and that it is safer, career-wise at least, to ask for directions from above. Employment and promotion generally depend on loyalty rather than skill or merit. All this favours conformity over creativity.

The government's key response to the challenge of bureaucratic reform has been to train and retrain cadres. This includes language and computer skills training, as well as the establishment of a National Institute of Administration, modelled on, and in cooperation with, the French École Nationale d'Administration. Given the authoritarian nature of the system, however, any serious attempt to change its culture will have to begin at its upper levels. Following the 2001 cabinet reshuffle, Asad directed cabinet ministers to define and broaden the responsibilities of assistant ministers, to appoint advisors and issue clear job descriptions for senior positions in their ministries. Ministers would, up to a point, be entitled to take decisions on investment and expenditure themselves, rather than submitting such plans to the prime minister. Cabinet ministers would be entitled to choose their own assistant ministers. Previously, such appointments had been the prerogative of the Ba'ath party's leadership.

Regional leadership

Such measures strengthened the authority of the ministers, the cabinet and state institutions at large, at the expense of the party. Under Hafiz al-Asad, the Ba'ath party had been turned into an instrument of the regime, rather than its motor. No general party congress took place between 1985 and 2000. The Ba'ath was the regime party, no doubt, but it did not control the regime. Effectively, it provided a mass basis and a vast patronage network.[34]

Bashar al-Asad inherited the party with the presidency. While he brought some allies into its 21-strong Regional (i.e., Syrian) Leadership, this body soon became the main stronghold of the regime conservatives. Although younger reform-minded party members support the president's reform agenda, the party apparatus still retains an element of conservatism and guarded scepticism with regard to any political or economic reform. Since Hafiz al-Asad's time, the party has lost the power to move things forward, but it can still block political progress – by vetoing decisions within the Regional Leadership, or simply by limiting their implementation in ministries, in public-sector firms and in the provinces. The president can overcome any veto on the leadership level, or he can force through a decision he wants if he deems it important enough: ultimately, leadership members do not want to lose their positions, and they do not want to put the authoritarian system as such in question by openly defying the president.[35] There is, however, little doubt that, for the modernisers' agenda to be implemented, the party's influence will have to be gradually reduced.

A debate about the role of the party emerged in early 2003, following and probably influenced by the installation of a new parliament, and by the Iraq war. The Ba'athist majority in parliament, the first one elected under the younger Asad, consisted largely of more reform-minded newcomers considered loyalists of the president, and the defeat of the Ba'athist regime in Iraq made it expedient to emphasise differences between the Syrian and the Iraqi branches of the party. This debate was settled with a widely publicised decision of the Regional Leadership that redefined the party's role under the constitution from 'leading' to 'planning and guidance, supervision and audit'. The party was not supposed to 'interfere with the work of the institutions, the directorates and the departments of the state'. Regime opponents deemed the decision insufficient, suggesting that a review of the constitutional clause that assigns a lead role to the party in the first place would have been more appropriate, and calling upon the regime to 'take the hands of the security agencies off the [state's] employment policies' if it really wanted to chose the best available personnel.[36] Yet Syria's official daily newspaper *Tishreen* may well have characterised the decision correctly as a 'juncture in the relation between the party and [state] power'. The move indicated that the balance within political structures had been tilted – a bit. Inasmuch as the capacity of Ba'athist functionaries to provide patronage was reduced, relatively at least, the weight of state institutions, and of the president, was increased.

In his inaugural speech, Bashar al-Asad explicitly stated that Syria would have to enter the 'century of institutions', and under his presidency a more institutionalised form of authoritarianism has emerged - a system that plays by the rules that it has itself defined, and reduces the interference of unauthorised organisations and individuals. This manifested itself in the way the regime dealt with dissent when it terminated the 'Damascus Spring': arrests and trials were reported in the local press, some trials were open to the public and to foreign observers, and public prosecutors and judges tried to give the impression of due process. Lawyers and human-rights organisations have also become more vocal. Yet this cannot hide the fact that the sentences handed down were of an arbitrary, political nature, and that the regime leadership continues to define the extent to which criticism and dissent will be tolerated. In short, the essential features of a state of institutions, notably the rule of law and an independent justice, remain absent.

Since Bashar al-Asad's accession, dissenters, modernisers and reform-minded regime loyalists have been debating whether the system is reformable from within. This debate has not been concluded. One positional difference is, however, clear: while dissenters, whether of a liberal-conservative or a more leftist complexion, emphasise political-structural reforms as inevitable conditions for the success of administrative and economic reform, for economic recovery and, eventually, to improve Syria's standing in the regional and international environment, the modernisers within the regime have clearly tried to separate the issues, and to concentrate on what they deem to be more easily achievable.[37]

Chapter 2

Economic Challenges and Policy Responses

Syria is not poor; rather, it is a middle-income, developing country that has not made the most efficient use of its resources. As is the case for many Arab and other oil-producing countries, Syria's ranking on the Human Development Index is lower than its per capita GDP would suggest: on the index, Syria is placed 110 out of 175, among countries like Vietnam, Tajikistan and Indonesia whose per capita incomes are much lower.[1] As the centre of the fertile crescent which extends from the Levant to the valleys of the Euphrates and the Tigris rivers, Syria has traditionally been an agricultural economy. Even today, some 30% of the workforce is employed in the agricultural sector, and agriculture accounts for a good quarter of the country's domestic product. Industrial development began with industries that make use of agricultural products. Textiles are the strongest and, theoretically at least, most competitive branch of manufacturing in Syria. Traditionally, due to its geographic location between the Mediterranean and Mesopotamia, Asia Minor and Arabia, trade has always been an important part of Syria's economy. Oil has been produced since 1958, but only became a major factor in the 1970s. Since the late 1980s, oil revenues have formed the largest part of Syria's foreign exchange earnings. The oil sector and manufacturing industries together employ some 13% of the workforce, and produce some 29% of GDP, around a quarter of which comes from manufacturing.[2]

During its short union with Egypt in 1958–62, and again, with more enduring and deeper effects, after the Ba'athist takeover in 1963,

Syria switched from a free-market to a state-controlled economy. The central elements were agricultural reform, which created a class of new small and medium landowners subject to central agricultural planning, the nationalisation of banks and major industrial companies, and the introduction of wide-ranging state controls over consumer prices, foreign trade, currency dealings and production. Following an import-substitution model, which many developing countries adhered to at the time, Syria also established a public industrial sector, which rapidly expanded with abundant financial aid from the Gulf monarchies in the 1970s. The Ba'athist leadership toyed with socialist ideas and slogans, particularly during the late 1960s, and imitated organisational models from the socialist countries of Eastern Europe. But it never put Syria on a Soviet-style course; a private sector always remained. The nationalisation of some medium-sized private companies was often meant to punish the enemies of the regime, rather than as part of a project to wipe out capitalism. Indeed, the state's distribution of oil income and Arab aid provided opportunities for private business. What emerged was a statist economy – marked by interventionism and heavy state control, and dependent on the state as the largest investor and entrepreneur.

From 1970, under the regime of Hafiz al-Asad, the economy was clearly seen as a handmaiden of politics. Asad was a pragmatist, not a socialist ideologue, and he made clear from the beginning that he wanted the private sector to contribute to national economic development. Generally, the ruling élite did not pay too much attention to economic and economic-policy issues per se unless economic crises threatened social or political stability. Consequently, when major trade and budget imbalances emerged in the mid-1980s, the Syrian government embarked on gradual and limited economic liberalisation (*infitah*). This culminated in the promulgation of an investment law (Law No. 10 of 1991) providing a range of incentives to foreign and expatriate investors. While the law should theoretically have been part of a more comprehensive reform process, it became, in fact, the last significant move on the economic-policy front for almost a decade.[3]

Partly as a result of these reforms (and partly due to increasing oil income), the Syrian economy picked up, and private-sector activity increased substantially. From the mid-1990s, however, the effects of the reforms evaporated; the government applied a strict austerity policy, and the economy stagnated. Austerity helped to cut budget deficits, stabilise the balance of payments and control inflation. Economic growth, however, fell behind population growth; per capita GDP became more or less static (see Table 1).[4]

Table 1: Syria: Basic Economic Indicators, 1981–2001

	Population (million)	GDP (US$bn)	Per capita GDP (US$)	Per capita GDP (LS, constant prices, 2000)
1981	9.05	15.50	1,712.71	51,776
1985	10.27	16.98	1,653.36	50,257
1990	12.12	12.30	1,014.85	42,138
1995	14.15	16.62	1,174.56	52,951
2000	16.32	17.33	1,061.89	55,389
2001	16.72	18.40	1,100.48	55,901

Source: Central Bureau of Statistics, Syrian Statistical Abstract 2002; http://www.worldbank.org/data/countrydata/aag/syr.aag.pdf; Arab Monetary Fund, Arab Countries: Economic Indicators, 1994–1984 and 1990–2000. Note that the enormous decrease of per capita GDP in US dollars between 1985 and 1990 is partly due to currency-rate calculations. Data compiled in Syrian currency, which still show a decline of more than 15%, may be more accurate.

Major challenges

Syria's new rulers, therefore, had good reasons to prioritise economic reform and modernisation. Challenges were manifold, and have generally been addressed more frankly since Bashar al-Asad's accession.

The first challenge was job creation. Population growth in Syria has slowed compared to the 1980s and 1990s, but still amounts to around 2.5% annually. The population is young: more than 40% are under 15 years of age, 52% are under 20. This implies enormous pressure on schools and universities, as well as on the labour market. Newcomers to this market are conservatively estimated at some 250,000 a year.[5] Unemployment is estimated at 20% overall, and this is probably higher among the younger generation.[6]

The second major challenge was Syria's dependence on oil revenues. Some 60–70% of the country's exports and foreign-exchange income, more than 12% of GDP, and some 50% of government revenue depend on oil.[7] Even if oil prices remain stable, oil income is likely to decrease: production has been falling from close to 600,000 barrels a day in the mid-1990s to some 525,000 due to the gradual depletion of oilfields; domestic consumption, which accounts for more than 40% of output, is increasing. Since Syria became a net oil exporter again in the late 1980s, Syrian officials have been complacent with regard to the foreseeable depletion of major oil fields, hoping instead for new discoveries and rising oil prices. Under Bashar al-Asad, this attitude has changed. New exploration contracts have been signed with international companies. In mid-2002, a deputy prime minister publicly acknowledged, for the first time, that Syria's oil production will not, in the medium term, be sufficient to finance development programmes.[8] Consequently, to create growth and stabilise the trade balance, Syria will have to increase its non-oil production and exports, particularly by renewing and expanding its industrial base. Agricultural production could still be diversified and increased, but the lack of abundant water resources would eventually limit growth in this sector.

The third major challenge was to encourage private capital. Syria's economy still has all the features of statism; it is dominated by the public sector, which controls essential industries such as oil and petrochemicals, electricity and steel production, as well as banking. The public sector accounts for about half of the output of manufacturing (non-oil) industries. It is overstaffed and as over-centralised as the rest of the administration. It is largely inefficient and makes heavy losses[9], and it also has to bear the interference of security and party agencies and large-scale corruption.[10] In the late 1980s and early 1990s, limited economic liberalisation aimed to encourage private investment, particularly in order to increase export-oriented production. The public sector suffered from the government's austerity policies and, as a result, the private sector gained in weight, absolutely as well as relative to the public sector. In 1991, the private industrial sector contributed less than half of the value added in the manufacturing industries. By 2001, this ratio had increased to over two-thirds.[11] The entire private sector accounts for an estimated 65% of GDP[12] and employs almost 75% of the workforce, compared to less than 70% a decade earlier.[13]

However, the state continued to interfere with private-sector activities in various ways, such as agricultural plans, import restrictions, currency regulations and a cumbersome bureaucracy.

There were no private banks and no stock market, and illegal currency dealing – a necessity for anyone who had to import raw material or machinery – could still be punished with up to 20 years in prison. The private economy remained organised in small-scale, family businesses. Larger private investments increased in response to the investment law of 1991, but slowed down in the second half of the decade. Syria's new leadership was clearly aware that the modernisation of the economy and the creation of jobs would have to be largely based on private Syrian, expatriate or foreign investment. In fact, Syrian investments in Arab countries outstripped Arab investments in Syria, which showed that Syria was one of the least attractive Arab countries.[14] Bashar al-Asad made clear that 'bad administration' and an outdated tax and banking system hampered private investment.[15] Three years into his regime, however, a proper investment climate, including issues such as governance and legal security, has yet to emerge.

A fourth challenge is social stability. While no reliable statistics exist, poverty and decreasing standards of human development have clearly become a problem over the 1980s and 1990s. Due to the austerity policies which the government applied throughout the 1990s, the number of people who are relatively poor has been increasing, and income differentials have widened. General and higher education have deteriorated as public spending on these sectors has decreased. Rising poverty affects levels of education as it leads to an increase in the number of drop-outs from school. Without an effective public social security system, schoolchildren have to contribute to the family income – some 10% of Syria's children between ten and 16 years of age are working for pay.[17] The unemployed and the poor are left to the care of their families or private social security associations. This functions well in the sense that there is little visible, absolute poverty – Syria's poor are not underfed and there are certainly fewer beggars on the streets of Damascus than there are in Washington DC. However, salient income differentials and the conspicuous consumption of the upper 5%, who are estimated to control some 50% of national income, contradict the alleged egalitarian orientation of the Ba'athist state. This might explain to some extent why the regime leadership was anxious to keep at least the semblance of statist or socialist features established under the Ba'ath, rather than doing away with them in the course of reform and alienating parts of their socio-political base, particularly in the trade and peasant union bureaucracy and in the party. Some of the reform team around Bashar al-Asad also feared that speedier reform steps would increase social problems, in the short run at least, and could trigger social unrest – which the new leadership could do without.

New approaches, old constraints

In his inaugural speech, Bashar al-Asad defined economic reform and modernisation as his highest priority, and left no doubt that economic policy and performance under his father's rule had not been satisfactory. 'Modernisation' became the key word: in particular, the new president mentioned the need to modernise the regulatory environment and the industrial base, activate and encourage the private sector, remove bureaucratic obstacles to investment, increase job opportunities, qualify cadres, improve education and expand information technology.[18] A series of laws and decrees was passed aimed at opening up the Syrian economy, encouraging private business and modernising administrative structures and education. Customs duties on imports for the local manufacturing industry were drastically cut, import restrictions, export taxes and limits on foreign-currency transactions were eased or removed and the possession of and trading in foreign currency were made no longer punishable by law. A tax-reform law, designed to reduce tax rates while increasing overall tax income, was brought to parliament. Based on the Chinese model, a law on so-called special economic zones for foreign investment was drafted. Employment offices were established for the first time, and the government set up an Agency for the Fight against Unemployment. This was to give financial support to public-sector projects that would create employment and give loans to young graduates to set up their own businesses. The establishment of private universities was permitted by law, and the Ministry of Higher Education created the National Institute for Administration and a Virtual University to connect students inside and outside the country to a worldwide network of higher-education institutes.

The most significant reform step was the promulgation in January 2001 of a banking law which permitted – for the first time since the nationalisation of 1963 – the establishment of private banks. Foreign capital was allowed to hold up to 49% of the stocks.

Consecutive laws introduced banking secrecy and reorganised the Central Bank. Given that Syria had not had experience with private banking for decades, it took time to set up the institutional framework and move through the licensing process. Among the difficulties for foreign banks seeking to set up business was the need to find Syrian investors prepared to contribute at least 51% of the shares. Expatriate capital remained cautious, often deciding to wait and see how serious and extensive economic reforms would be.[19] Eventually, one Jordanian and two Lebanese banks obtained authorisations to go ahead; in January 2004, the first private bank opened its doors.

The decision to allow private banks was a strong signal of reform. However, it would hardly serve its purpose unless it became the cornerstone of a comprehensive effort to reform the economic system. Banking reform was indicative, in many respects, of the impediments facing the reform process at large. There were divergent views within Bashar al-Asad's team over the scope of reform. Some younger members of the élite believed that Syria should state its commitment to free-market development clearly, while others wanted to maintain as much state control as possible. The result was often a compromise that failed to convince domestic and international observers that Syria was indeed on the path of reform. Bureaucratic, legal and political obstacles hindered even those reform steps that the political leadership had, in principle, agreed upon.

Conflicting views, practical obstacles

There was little disagreement that, without a return to economic growth, Syria would not be able to cope with the problem of unemployment. Equally, there was little disagreement that, in order to enhance growth, the private sector would have to be given more space. There was also broad agreement that administrative reform, education and technical modernisation were priority issues. For the president's reform team the latter was centrally, and symbolically, about increasing computer literacy and the spread of the internet. By the beginning of 2003, only an estimated 1.45% of all Syrians used the internet, an extremely low penetration level even by regional standards.[20] The government began to introduce computer lessons in schools, planned for the local production of affordable personal computers and announced its intention to raise connectivity to at least 5% of the population. Prohibitive connection costs were reduced and internet cafés licensed.[21] Objections from the security establishment that had kept the spread of communication technologies in check could be overcome since the technocrats had the full support of the president. However, this did not prevent the security services from interfering; in 2003, for example, access to certain e-mail sites was suddenly blocked.[22]

There was also broad agreement within the regime élite that a more expansive fiscal policy should be followed to help bring the country back to growth. The austerity policy of the 1990s was effectively scrapped. Budget increases ranged between 10% and 18% in the three years following Bashar al-Asad's accession. Higher deficits were tolerated.[23] The relative decrease in expenditure on education was reversed, and some of the real income losses that those employed by the state had suffered over the 1990s were offset by two consecutive pay rises of 25% and 20% in 2001 and 2002. Further pay rises were contemplated to bring state salaries – averaging LS6,000 ($120) a month in 2003 – to more acceptable levels. Credit became more easily available from state-run banks, and the newly established Council for Credit and Finance lowered interest rates in 2003 to encourage private investment (the first time interest rates had been cut for more than 20 years).[24]

Two other issues were more controversial and underlined the intra-élite differences that remained on Syria's economic development path. These were an association agreement with the European Union (EU), and privatisation. Negotiations on an association agreement with the EU under the so-called Barcelona process or Euro-Mediterranean Partnership[25] began in 1998. The EU is by far Syria's most important trading partner, and any agreement would essentially be about free trade and aid: it would improve access for Syrian products to the European market, and force Syria to lower and eventually remove barriers to European imports. An agreement would also contain a reference to human rights and democracy, something Syria and other Arab governments did not reject, but certainly regarded as illegitimate interference in domestic affairs. According to a rare opinion poll conducted in 2001, a clear majority of Syrians expected positive effects to flow from an association agreement with the EU.[26] However, some among Syria's political élite doubted the desirability of such an agreement. Sceptics argued that Syria would not benefit from mutual trade liberalisation, particularly as long as the EU maintained restrictions on agricultural imports. Muhammad Atrash, an economist who became Syria's finance minister in the cabinet reshuffle of 2001, argued shortly before his appointment that an association with the EU would constitute a threat to Arab industries and to Arab efforts to achieve economic unity.[27] The majority among the new economic-policy team, however, was generally in favour of an agreement, considering it the safest way to manoeuvre Syria into globalisation. While there would be losses in the short term, openness to the outside world and reform of domestic administrative and industrial structures would eventually be both beneficial and unavoidable. Why not, therefore, accept European support?[28]

While reservations remained with regard to potential European interference in domestic politics, Syria's leadership eventually decided, early in 2002, to speed up the negotiations. The decision was clearly reflected in public discourse: rather than highlighting potential risks to domestic industry, members of the political élite, as well as the state-run media, focused on the positive effects of an association with the EU. For example, Syria's then minister of industry, an ideologically more left-leaning member of the reform team, stressed that Syria, due to its special and independent path, did not have to take lessons from anybody, certainly not from the EU, the World Bank or the IMF. However, reform, modernisation and the rehabilitation of the industrial sector were urgent, and an association agreement would provide 'millions of Euros' in aid for that purpose. Syria should therefore prepare the ground for successful negotiations.[29] Given the statist nature of Syria's economic system, this was not easy. Negotiations for an agreement took considerably longer than for other Mediterranean countries; they were eventually finalised in December 2003. The devil often lay in the detail. Thus, in early 2003, a major practical obstacle seemed to have been removed with a government decision to replace general import bans for certain goods by a system of tariffs whose gradual reduction over a limited period would then be negotiated with the EU. Given that import bans had been imposed or lifted on thousands of product types in a rather ad hoc manner for more than 40 years, those in charge of the file were simply overwhelmed by the task – proving unable to produce the comprehensive list of tariffs that was to be the basis for detailed negotiation foreseen for July of that year.

While Asad made very clear that he wanted the talks to succeed as soon as possible, the negotiation round had to be postponed for three months.

In contrast to its decision to pursue an EU association agreement, the Syrian leadership decided against privatising parts of the public sector. Instead, public-sector reform was to be promoted, and foreign companies could, if necessary, be put in charge of public-sector companies on a contract basis. But no state firms would be dismantled or sold; the industrial public sector would be 'rationalised', while the state would maintain an entrepreneurial role in 'strategic' as well as 'profitable' fields.[30] Government representatives emphasised the risk of social unrest were privatisation to cause major redundancies, and spoke of the need to maintain the public sector for 'strategic and security' reasons: as long as Syria expected potential Israeli aggression, the state should be able to secure the supply of basic goods through its own industries.[31] Privatisation of parts of the state sector would also directly affect powerful vested interests. Despite being loss-making, the public sector remained an important instrument for patronage, political mobilisation and control; it also offered ample opportunities for illegal enrichment.[32] Furthermore, an open decision in favour of privatisation would constitute a clear break with Ba'athist ideology, and would antagonise a substantial part of the party and a large number of trade-union functionaries.

The pace of reform

Generally, Syria's political leadership adopted a gradualist approach to the scope and speed of economic reform. Reform was openly defined as a goal, but would be introduced piecemeal so as not to upset the domestic balance. This approach, while perhaps politically expedient, risked seeing Syria fall further behind other regional states that competed with it for the same investors and trading partners. Things moved, but they moved far too slowly for those who were convinced of the need of substantial reform. 'Before Bashar al-Asad took over,' Elias Samao, a politics professor from Aleppo University, put it in a conversation with the author, 'Syria was a turtle on its back. Now it's a turtle back on its feet.'

By advancing in such a gradualist manner, the Syrian leadership did not give a clear message to potential investors or foreign partners as to where it wanted to lead the country. Thus, while the first private banks were given licences, it was still not clear if and when they would be allowed to trade in foreign currency. Reflecting compromises within the regime élite, such policies kept foreign as well as domestic observers wondering whether any strategic reform decision beyond the modernisation of statism had actually been taken. Intra-élite differences are part of the explanation for this approach. Another part is explained by bureaucratic resistance, to which the president himself has alluded.[33] The accumulation of four decades of statism presents its own problems: the compiling of a system of tariffs, referred to above, is just one case in point. Property rights are often unclear or disputed. One example that concerned the Minister of Agriculture pertained to Syria's largely defunct state farms, whose land had de facto been taken over by individual farmers. While the minister would have liked to dissolve the farms, such a step would raise more than simply technical problems. Aside from farmers who had 'laid their hands' on the land, as the Syrian expression for such tolerated practice goes, there were also its former owners who had been expropriated on the basis of a 1958 land reform law but, contrary to the law, had never actually been compensated. Any decision to sell or redistribute the land would upset social and political balances, and even risk rural or tribal violence. It was more simple to leave things as they were.[34]

Corruption and the lack of accountability remain a major disincentive to local and foreign investors. While some officials have been dismissed from their jobs or brought to court on charges of corruption or mismanagement, this anti-corruption campaign lacks credibility as long as well-connected individuals, including members of Asad's wider family, seem above the law. The most prominent case is that of the president's cousin, Rami Makhlouf, who has become a business tycoon of the new era. Makhlouf controls SyriaTel, one of the country's two mobile-phone companies, and has important interests in duty-free shops at Syria's airports and land borders, private schools, refuse collection in Damascus and the import of cigarettes. Makhlouf's businesses were generally well managed, and a firm like SyriaTel can be considered part of the drive to modernise Syria. However, Makhlouf was able to acquire monopolies or quasi-monopolies in lucrative business fields without any competition. There is no independent judiciary that would guarantee the rights of Makhlouf's business partners in case of dispute. An exemplary case was that of Orascom Telecom, an Egyptian company that initially held a 25% stake in SyriaTel. In 2002, when financial disagreements arose between the Egyptian and Syrian partners, a Syrian court froze Orascom's assets in Syria. Orascom was able to secure a court ruling in its favour outside Syria, and the two sides eventually agreed on an 'amicable' solution that ended Orascom's partnership in SyriaTel.[35] The damage to Syria's image as a potential location for foreign investment, however, had already been done. If an Egyptian company with good knowledge of the intricacies of doing business in the Middle East was not able to prevail in the Syrian market, international investors are unlikely to be optimistic about their prospects.

Finally, there is the political dimension of economic reform: progressive economic liberalisation would sooner or later shift the domestic balance of power. Demands would increase for political change or, at least, for establishing and guaranteeing transparency, the rule of law and, more generally, 'better governance'. For parts of the regime élite, this remains a threatening prospect.

The economic importance of regional politics

Syria's economic condition and the welfare of its people have always been heavily dependent on regional politics. Thus, the increase in Arab aid payments after 1973, their decrease over the 1980s, and their renewed expansion in the first half of the 1990s was largely connected to Syria's policies and position in the region.[36] Job opportunities in the Gulf Arab countries have equally depended, partly at least, on Syria's relations with these states, and trade with neighbouring and other regional countries has often been subject to bilateral conflict. Exports to Turkey, for example, were affected by a crisis over Syria's support for the Kurdish separatist PKK in the second half of the 1990s; the Syrian-Jordanian border was closed several times during the same period because of differences over policy towards Israel; and the Syrian-Iraqi border was sealed for most of the 1980s and 1990s due to the political conflict between Damascus and Baghdad.

Even from a purely economic perspective, therefore, it was reasonable that Bashar al-Asad and his government made conscious efforts to improve Syria's relations with its neighbours. The most significant move was the gradual opening to Iraq, begun under Hafiz al-Asad but speeded up under his son, a decision as much of economic importance as political consequence. While exact figures are unavailable, Syria's positive growth rates in 2000–02 were probably largely due to the Iraq factor. From late 2000, when the Kirkuk-Banias pipeline came on stream after two decades' closure, to the US invasion of Iraq in March 2003, Syria was both the main route for Iraqi oil exports outside the UN-controlled oil-for-food agreement, and a main supplier to the Iraqi market. 'Unofficial' shipments through the Iraqi-Syrian pipeline totalled some 150–200,000 barrels per day, allowing Syria to increase its own oil exports by the same amount.[37] As Syria reportedly received these deliveries at two-thirds of their market value, the deal generated $800 million to $1,300m a year. At the same time, Syria's private sector experienced a boom thanks to Iraqi purchases from the Syrian market conducted partly under, and partly outside, the oil-for-food agreement. Iraq made Syria its main supplier, at least for products legally imported, directly or by transit, under the sanctions regime. Syrian experts put total exports to Iraq at $2bn in 2002, including Syrian consumer products and transit goods purchased and resold by Syrian traders.[38] This figure, if correct, would add some 40% to Syria's total registered exports.[39]

At the time of writing, the economic consequences of the Iraq war for the Syrian economy were not fully visible, though it is likely that the loss of subsidised Iraqi oil would reduce Syria's state income by up to 15% of the official budget.[40] The loss of Iraqi oil rents would reduce the president's patronage capacity: this had been freely disposable income, to support the budget, sponsor social programmes or pay rises, import goods outside the budget or simply buy loyalties. Following the war, Syria's private industrial sector maintained much of the trade relationship established with Iraq in the preceding years. It was clear, though, that Syrians would no longer enjoy privileged access to the Iraqi market. On the other hand, the loss of rent income and of privileged, non-competitive markets could create an incentive to make Syrian industry more competitive, and the economy at large more efficient. The need is there, but so too are the constraints that have slowed the economic and administrative reforms which Bashar al-Asad has made his priorities.

Chapter 3

Coping with External Challenges

When Bashar al-Asad assumed the presidency, the regional and international environment did not appear overly threatening. Overall, the new president received a positive though sometimes sceptical welcome from Syria's neighbours and foreign partners. Syrian–Israeli negotiations had ground to a halt after talks in December 1999 and January 2000, and a failed meeting between Hafiz al-Asad and US President Bill Clinton in March. Even though both Israelis and Syrians expected to resume their talks, there was no feeling of urgency: Israeli Prime Minister Ehud Barak ended Israel's occupation in Southern Lebanon and began to concentrate his energies on the Palestinian track, and Syria was occupied with the presidential succession.

If Bashar al-Asad hoped for a period of calm, he was to be disappointed. Hardly a month after his inauguration, the Israeli-Palestinian-American summit at Camp David failed. Two months later, the second Palestinian *intifada* began; another four months saw Ariel Sharon elected Israel's prime minister. During Bashar al-Asad's second year in office, the 11 September terrorist attacks on New York and Washington shook the world, sent their shock waves back to the Middle East and precipitated a new, more aggressive US policy towards the region. Asad's third year was marked by the Iraq crisis and war. This has been the greatest challenge for his regime so far. Syria's policies in the crisis have had serious implications for its relations with the US. The war and its outcome have also had domestic effects.

In foreign and security policy, Asad largely relied on his father's former advisors. While the members of his economic-reform team looked up to him, this was not necessarily the case with these long-term foreign-policy experts: they accepted him as president, but at times seem to have enjoyed showing him his lack of experience – rather than always giving him their best advice.

Patterns, interests and capabilities

To claim that the foreign policy of a given regime follows a particular pattern is always an analytical simplification. At the same time, the identification of such patterns may help to understand the cognitive and conceptual framework in which foreign and security-policy decisions are actually taken. In this sense, it can be said that, throughout his 30-year rule, Hafiz al-Asad concentrated his energy on the 'struggle for the Middle East' (to paraphrase the title of Patrick Seale's work), basically viewing it as a contest with Israel. His approach was pragmatic, in that ideological motives were never allowed to overrule calculations of interests and capabilities. The economy and other domestic issues, however, became a handmaiden of regional policies.[1] Nonetheless, even opposition figures have generally lauded Hafiz al-Asad's foreign-policy record, and his successor has sought to demonstrate continuity in this field. This includes a stark, though not always convincing, insistence on the independence of Syrian foreign policy from external pressures or demands.

At the same time, a change of pattern has emerged: Bashar al-Asad and his team give priority to modernisation, and they are prepared to use regional and international politics to secure domestic interests. Practically, this implies two partly contradictory features. First, as the new team has a good understanding of the economic function of regional and international relations, it has sought to put foreign policy to the service of the country's economic recovery. In contrast to his father's men, Bashar al-Asad's team also understands, in principle at least, the need to engage in public diplomacy, particularly with the United States. For the first time, there are now people in the foreign ministry and in Syria's Washington embassy who can explain the country's positions through well-worded opinion pieces, who can talk to the press and make convincing appearances on American television. Second, the new leadership team has sought to use foreign policy to enhance the president's popularity. This has been successful with regard to the domestic audience, but has often irritated other regional and international players.

Within this framework, Syria's vital foreign and security-policy interests have not changed. The Arab-Israeli conflict remains the main concern. Since the Madrid peace conference in 1991, the prime objective has been to reach an 'honourable' settlement. This includes not only the return of Israeli-occupied territory, but also an acceptable outcome on the Israeli-Palestinian track and the preclusion of Israeli hegemony in a post-conflict Middle East. Lebanon, in particular, must preserve its pro-Syrian stability, lest it fall under Israeli influence.[2] Generally, Syria's approach to Arab-Israeli issues is driven by a zero-sum logic which holds that Israeli gains in terms of security, economic resources or political relations constitute a relative loss for the Arab side.

Syria's political élite is well aware that Syria could not be defended in the event of an all-out military confrontation with Israel. Sheer numbers do not represent the actual balance of forces: while Syria has a huge conscript army, its technical standards are far below that of Israel's armed forces, and much of its hardware is in a poor state of maintenance.[3] The expert assumption on both sides is that, in case of war, Israel's air force would rapidly gain control of the skies, and Israeli armour would be on the outskirts of Damascus before Syrian troops could enter Israeli territory. At best, Syrian forces might be able to launch a surprise attack on Israeli installations in the occupied Syrian territories – the Golan Heights and Mount Hermon/Jabal al-Sheikh – and Syrian *Scud* missiles could hit Israeli cities. This does not make for an offensive capability that could seriously threaten Israel. Moreover, Syria has neither a nuclear deterrent nor - since the end of the Soviet Union at least – a potent international ally. Syria has opted to strengthen its air defences and to build a chemical-weapons and ballistic-missile capacity as a deterrent.[4] It has also sought to instrumentalise the 'Lebanese resistance', i.e. the armed presence of Hizbollah in the south of Lebanon. While Hizbollah's combat operations have been reduced to almost zero since before the Iraq war, Syria wants to maintain the organisation as a means of putting pressure on Israel.

Given its centrality in Syria's security perception, the conflict with Israel has an enormous bearing on Syria's foreign relations in general. While other criteria and interests play a role, Syrian policy-makers and diplomats tend to view relations with third countries largely in terms of how their policies impact upon the regional balance of forces, and what these countries can contribute to a resolution of the conflict. This is of particular importance for Syrian-American relations. Most of Syria's political élite deplores US support for Israel, and shares with the general public a deep suspicion of US policies in the region. They also know, however, that an acceptable settlement with Israel will only come about under US sponsorship. The Iraq war has added another challenging dimension to this ambivalent relationship: the fact that the US has virtually become Syria's neighbour to the east is enormously disturbing - and makes it all the more important to maintain a working relationship with the US administration. Overall, events related to the Arab-Israeli conflict, Iraq and bilateral relations with the US have occupied the Syrian leadership much more during Bashar al-Asad's first three years in office than had been anticipated. This does not, however, mean that relations with other states in the neighbourhood or with Europe did not matter.

European opportunities

The need to put Syria's foreign relations to the service of economic recovery and modernisation has meant cultivating relations with the EU and its member states, and making best use of regional opportunities for trade and cooperation. Bashar al-Asad did not initially expect much of a political contribution from Europe – the EU did not even figure in his inaugural speech. However, in his first year in office he travelled to Spain, France and Germany, with economic issues high on the agenda. The Syrian government resolved long-standing debt problems with France and Germany, thereby removing a major obstacle to European development assistance. As outlined in Chapter 2, the new leadership also took negotiations for an association agreement with the EU more seriously than its predecessor. This reflected a shift in Syria's approach to dealing with Europe's regional initiatives. In 1995, Syria had entered the Barcelona process for mainly political reasons. Primarily, Damascus hoped that a more active Europe would balance US influence in the Middle East. Today, Syrian decision-makers consider the economic benefits of partnership more seriously.

Sometimes conflicting approaches exist within the Syrian élite. The president and his modernisers are generally convinced that Europe can help Syria to address globalisation in a more benign way. Conservatives and older foreign-policy hands are more prepared to subject relations with the EU to an often highly symbolic form of regional politics. Syria stayed away from the Euro-Mediterranean meetings of foreign ministers in Marseilles, Brussels and Valencia in 2000, 2001 and 2002, and made Lebanon do the same. It was 'illogical', Foreign Minister Farouq al-Sharaa explained, that 'the Israeli foreign minister is having dinner with us while people are being killed in Palestine'.[5] As is often the case, Syrian diplomacy had made a point, rather than trying to win support for its point of view. Only after the Iraq war did Syria (and Lebanon) decide to reverse their empty-chair policy. Both countries participated in the May 2003 Euro-Mediterranean foreign ministers conference in Crete. Under strong American pressure over its position in and after the war, Syria's leadership clearly realised that it needed friends. At the same time, Asad decided to speed up the negotiations for the association agreement – wisely so, as the Europeans made no secret of the fact that they might lose interest. In May 2003, EU Commission president Romano Prodi suggested that Syria was about to become the 'odd man out' among Europe's Mediterranean partners.[6]

While the association agreement is mainly about economic cooperation, political issues have never been absent from Syria's relations with the EU. Modernisers and conservatives alike have been uneasy with European calls for political change, fearful that democracy and human-rights clauses in an association agreement would lead to what the regime characterises as illegitimate interference in its domestic affairs.[7] Conversely, representatives of both trends call for a stronger European political role in the peace process. Syrian leaders understand that the EU is neither able nor willing to replace the US as the main peace broker, even when US administrations do not fulfil that function. They do, however, sense that Europe would make an effort at least to guarantee that Syria would not be left out if Palestinians and Israelis were actually to proceed along the international 'Road map' for the Middle East peace process. Given that Syria might expect increasing American pressure, strong relations with Europe and individual EU states – Britain in particular – could become vital.[8]

Neighbourhood matters

While Europe is Syria's main trading partner, Syria is still integrated into its regional environment: some 15% to 20% of its registered exports and imports are with other Arab states, about twice the general average of intra-regional trade in the Middle East, and another 6% or so is accounted for by Turkey.[9] Other than Syria's exports to Europe and other industrialised countries, which consist almost exclusively of oil and oil products, the regional market takes most of Syria's non-oil exports. Therefore, Syria's private sector has a greater stake in these exchanges, and the relevance for industrial development and employment generation is enormous. Syria's new leadership has demonstrated that it takes the economic dimension of regional relations more seriously than its predecessors. This means, in particular, not allowing political differences over regional issues to disrupt functional cooperation. Relations with Jordan and Turkey are cases in point.

Depoliticising relations with Jordan

Under Hafiz al-Asad and King Hussein, economic relations between Syria and Jordan often suffered from highly personalised political differences. Syria's new leadership has also been unhappy with Jordan's policies, particularly its maintenance of close diplomatic and trade relations with Israel during the second *intifada*. Both Bashar al-Asad and Hussein's successor King Abdullah, however, have been pragmatic, trying to push common economic interests despite political disagreements. Among other things, the electricity networks between Syria, Jordan, Egypt and Lebanon were connected, Syria has delivered water to Jordan in dry summers, and the foundation stones for a long-overdue joint dam project (the Wahda dam on the Yarmouk river) were eventually laid early in 2004.

Syria's new leaders have also made an effort to use private-sector representatives in foreign relations, thereby supporting the image of a more open, more pragmatic country. While Syrian government officials stayed away from the World Economic Forum regional meeting in Amman in June 2003 – Syria does not approve of any Arab–Israeli 'normalisation' steps in the absence of a comprehensive peace or serious steps towards it – the meeting was attended by a business delegation led by Ratib al-Shallah, the president of the Federation of Syrian Chambers of Commerce.

Seeking common interests with Turkey

Relations with Turkey began to improve under Hafiz al-Asad,

following a near-breakdown in 1998, when Turkey massed troops on the Syrian border and threatened military action unless Syria ended its support for the Kurdish PKK. Faced with a possible invasion, Syria expelled PKK leader Abdullah Öcalan and signed the so-called Adana agreement, a capitulation of sorts that committed Syria to cease all support for Kurdish rebels.[10] Thereafter, relations between the two countries improved. Bashar al-Asad's government has maintained this momentum. Trade has picked up steadily. In 2002, the Syrian and Turkish chiefs of staff concluded a military-cooperation agreement that includes joint exercises. In July 2003, Turkey agreed to resume talks over Euphrates water, a vital Syrian concern, which Turkey had occasionally used as a means of exerting pressure during the 1990s. In January 2004, Bashar al-Asad undertook a highly successful state visit to Ankara. Agreements on industrial and energy cooperation were concluded; confidence-building measures on borders agreed; and Turkey offered its good offices to mediate between Syria and Israel. Syria has to all intents and purposes accepted Turkish sovereignty over Hatay. Even though Syrian maps still show the province of Iskanderun, as it is called in Arabic, as part of Syria, active irredentism has ceased.

As with Jordan, improving relations with Turkey also meant that Syria would have to accept that its neighbours choose their regional alignments according to their own, and not Syria's, agenda. While Syria could not be expected to appreciate Turkey's military cooperation with Israel,[11] the challenge was to pursue fruitful cooperation regardless – rather than adding to Turkish suspicions of Syria, thereby indirectly further entrenching Ankara's alliance with Tel Aviv. Of course, Turkey and Syria also have common political concerns, particularly over the future of Iraq. Syrians were impressed that Turkey refused to support the US invasion of Iraq, and neither Turkey nor Syria or Iran is interested in the establishment of too-autonomous a Kurdish entity.[12]

Iran, Saudi Arabia and Egypt

Iran, Saudi Arabia and Egypt represented the corner-stones of Hafiz al-Asad's regional diplomacy. With Iran, the elder Asad built an alliance that included Syrian support during the Iran–Iraq war, Iranian economic support and cooperation in Lebanon.[13] Egypt and Saudi Arabia gave Syria a political-strategic depth. They supported

Syria's stance in the peace process, and refrained from undermining its position in Lebanon. Syria was one of the main recipients of bilateral Saudi as well as Kuwaiti aid. Syria coordinated its policies towards Iraq with Riyadh and Kuwait, and accepted a measure of Saudi influence in Lebanese affairs. The leaderships of the three countries were all aware that, as long as they coordinated their policies, which they did quite well over the 1990s, they would be able to dominate the Arab League and the agenda of intra-Arab politics.[14]

Under Bashar al-Asad, relations with these countries have remained important, as early visits to their capitals and an intensive exchange of visitors demonstrate. Iran remains an ally: it is strongly involved in Lebanon, but seems to accept the priority of Syrian interests and Syria's wish to reach a settlement with Israel. Saudi Arabia no longer provides as much financial help to Syria as it did in the 1980s and 1990s, but it is an important market for Syrian products, a main source of foreign investment for Syria and a trusted partner whose advice the Syrian élite is prepared to take. Relations with Egypt have been more complicated. Intensive diplomatic contacts, including frequent summits, have been maintained. Meetings between Hosni Mubarak and Bashar al-Asad, however, appear to be held more to address recurrent misunderstandings and differences than to devise a common regional agenda. Personal factors have also played a role. Asad and his team felt, correctly it seems, that Mubarak did not really take the young president seriously. The Egyptian leader was offended by demonstrations in Damascus against his regime, which the Syrian authorities did nothing to prevent, and by the harsh, populist rhetoric that Asad used at Arab League meetings. Asad's denouncement of Arab regimes that were not willing to cut relations with Israel, clearly directed at Egypt as well as Jordan, may have endeared him to the anti-regime opposition, but certainly not to the Egyptian president.[15] Syria's relations with Egypt were also affected by disagreements about how to deal with the Iraqi issue.

Iraq and the American threat

After almost two decades of enmity between the Syrian and Iraqi regimes, during which Syria supported Iran in the 1980–88 Iraq–Iran war and provided troops in the coalition effort to liberate Kuwait in 1991, relations began to thaw by 1997. The UN oil-for-food programme for Iraq came into effect, and Syrian industrialists started to lobby for an opening towards Iraq. Iraq's need for cheap consumer goods, the ability of Syrian industry to produce them and geographic proximity offered enormous opportunities for Syria's recession-plagued economy, particularly for the private sector.

After Bashar al-Asad's accession, relations improved much faster. The main motive for the Syrian leadership was to further economic interests and draw a financial rent. The railway link to Iraq was re-established, trade exchanges were increased and, in the latter part of 2000, the Iraq–Syria oil pipeline was reopened. Syria, considering the interests of Arab allies and friends such as Saudi Arabia and Kuwait, refused Iraq's demand for a full restoration of diplomatic relations, but interest sections under Algerian auspices were opened in Damascus and Baghdad. At the same time, some Syrian leaders began to speak of Iraq as Syria's 'strategic depth'. From 2001, ministerial visits became almost routine. Consequently, Syria did not even try to create the impression that it would support the Bush administration's initial efforts to rejuvenate sanctions against Iraq, or its more aggressive line following the terrorist attacks of 11 September 2001.

In fact, Syria followed a dual strategy. On the one hand, it cooperated with the US on international terrorism, particularly through the exchange of information and by allowing US investigators access to suspects in Syrian jails. Syrian cooperation in this field was repeatedly lauded by US officials.[16] Asad and his collaborators underlined that Syria, while distinguishing terrorism from legitimate acts of resistance against foreign occupation, shared with the US an interest in fighting al-Qaeda and international terrorism. On the other hand, the Syrian leadership left no doubt that it rejected overall US policies in the region, and would do its part to ward off a US-led war on Iraq. As the only Arab member on the UN Security Council in 2002 and 2003, Syria occupied a prominent place in the crisis leading up to the Iraq war. It voted with UN Security Council Resolution 1441 in November 2002, but only after receiving guarantees that it implied no automatic sanction for war. Consequently, Syria rejected the idea of a second resolution that would have legitimised the war. Even within the Arab context, Syria's position came closest to openly supporting Baghdad.

Domestically, the leadership's pro-Iraqi stance went down well with a public clearly both pro-Iraqi and anti-American.

Internationally, however, Syria came under pressure. US and Israeli leaders accused Damascus of supporting the Iraqi war effort, shipping military technology to the Iraqi army, giving a haven to Iraqi officials and even allowing Iraq to store weapons of mass destruction (WMD) on Syrian territory. Although Iraq did indeed import military equipment through Syria in the months before the war, there is no indication that Syria agreed to hide WMD on behalf of the Iraqi regime. Suspicious truck movements from Iraq before the war – which US satellites are likely to have spotted – were in fact civilian in nature, though still illegal.[17] However, Syria did allow Arab volunteers to cross into Iraq, including hundreds of Syrians, many of whom did not return. Asad and his associates left little doubt that they wished the US army to be defeated, or at least not to gain an easy victory.[18] In fact, the Syrian leadership gravely misread the military situation and the ability of the Iraqi regime to resist: Baghdad fell much earlier and with much less resistance than had been expected. Syria's official media did not report the toppling of the statues of Saddam Hussein on 9 April 2003.

Syria suddenly found itself in a completely new geostrategic situation, sandwiched between Israel to the south and a US-dominated Iraq to the east. Only Lebanon remained an ally – at least as long as it remained under Syrian tutelage. With its pro-Iraq stance and its denouncement of Arab states that had explicitly supported, or acquiesced in, the US-led war against Iraq, the Syrian leadership had offended Egypt and lost much sympathy in Kuwait, one of the country's main financial supporters. Fears grew, more so among the public than among officials, that the US might now turn on Damascus, with part of its military power already present on Syria's long border with Iraq. The US Army had cut the Iraqi oil pipeline to Syria, and the 'Syria Accountability and Lebanese Sovereignty Act' was reintroduced in the US Congress in May and signed into law by President Bush in December 2003.[19] Military measures were not ruled out if Syria failed to comply with US demands related to Iraq and to the Arab-Israeli conflict. Primarily, Syria should stay away from Iraq and not give refuge to individuals from the former Iraqi regime; it should close down the offices of radical Palestinian organisations in Damascus and expel their leadership; and it should not interfere with the implementation of the so-called 'roadmap' for Israeli-Palestinian peace. With considerably less emphasis, the US also demanded that Syria disarm Lebanon's *Hizbollah* and withdraw its troops from Lebanon.

The Syrian leadership sought to make the best of a situation that it clearly could not appreciate. If parts of the regime had toyed with the idea of actively supporting militant Iraqi resistance against the US-led occupation, the idea was quickly laid to rest in view of US threats and pressure. Reluctantly, Syria agreed to cooperate with the US and the new Iraqi authorities in freezing and eventually repatriating assets of the former Iraqi regime in Syrian bank accounts. The border with Iraq was closed to Iraqi refugees,[20] although border crossings were held open to the movement of trade and visitors, both by Syria and by US forces on the Iraqi side, and trade exchanges resumed shortly after the war. Although Syria probably could not control its borders with Iraq to a degree that would have prevented every Arab who sought to join the anti-American resistance from crossing, the government no longer encouraged such jihadist tourism. It seems, however, that individual officers at the border facilitated the traffic of such fighters for a bribe.

Politically, Syria's leadership left no doubt that it would remain opposed to the occupation of Iraq. Media comment to the effect that the real war aims of the US had been the 'Israelisation of the Middle East, the Americanisation of the oil, and the destruction of Arab nationalism'[21] expressed a widespread feeling among the public and the political élite. While it did not directly support Iraqi resistance to the occupation, Damascus was clearly not unhappy to see the Americans encounter unexpected difficulties. Officially, Syria tried to steer a pragmatic course: it demanded an end to the occupation, but declared its consent to Security Council Resolution 1483, which acknowledged the occupation, and voted with Resolution 1511, which practically gave a UN mandate to US-led forces. Syria did not explicitly recognise the Governing Council which the Coalition Authority in Iraq appointed, but in practice it accepted the Council members as de facto representatives of Iraq and began to cooperate with the new Iraqi authorities on issues such as the reopening of the Aleppo–Mosul rail link. The Syrian government hinted at the possibility of sending troops to participate in a multilateral force for Iraq if it was under UN command, and to help in reconstruction efforts if there was a clear timetable for US withdrawal.[22]

Despite occasional fierce denouncements of US policies by individual officials, Syria's leadership sought to preserve a line of communication with Washington. The government also made efforts to improve Syria's image in the US, engaging in dialogue with US politicians and think-tanks, and attempted to attract US business interests. The signing, in June 2003, of an oil and gas exploration agreement with two US companies was generally seen as significant.[23] Syrian decision-makers clearly hoped that such deals would contribute to a mood of cooperation with Syria. Asad and his team are aware that they need to maintain good relations with the US not only to avoid a costly confrontation, but mainly because of the role that Damascus still expects Washington to play in its main foreign and security policy concern: the unresolved conflict with Israel.

The 'Strategic Option' on hold: Syria and the peace process

Syria has been a key player in the Arab-Israeli conflict. It fought Israel in four wars, and parts of its territory, the Golan Heights and Mount Hermon, have been under Israeli occupation since 1967. Following the 1973 war, Syria regained a small part of this territory through a US-brokered disengagement treaty. While the Syrian-Israeli front has since been quiet, repeated military confrontations have taken place in Lebanon, either directly, as during Israel's 1982 invasion, or by proxy, mainly through Syria's support of Hizbollah's guerrilla war against Israeli occupation.

Syria has also been an essential participant in the Middle East peace process initiated at the Madrid conference of 1991. It did not take part in the so-called Multilaterals (the multilateral working groups on regional issues that emerged from the conference), but linked possible participation to progress on the bilateral Syrian–Israeli track. Negotiations with Israel became the main policy issue occupying Hafiz al-Asad almost until his death in June 2000.[24] Serious direct and indirect negotiations between the two countries were first held under the government of Yitzhak Rabin (1992–95) and continued under Shimon Peres (1995–96), mostly with active and indispensable US involvement. These talks did not result in a declaration of principles, but they left both sides with a clearer understanding of each other's position, and what the Syrians have called the 'Rabin deposit' – a conditional or at least 'hypothetical'

(Rabinovich), but 'unequivocal' (Zisser), statement by Rabin of his readiness for an eventual Israeli withdrawal to the lines of 4 June 1967.[25] The 'contours' of an agreement (Rabinovich) had also become clear: full Israeli withdrawal (wherever the exact border line eventually would be), mutually-agreed security arrangements, an agreement over water flows from the Golan Heights into the Jordan valley, and the normalisation of bilateral relations. Even during the premiership of Benjamin Netanyahu, while no official talks were held, indirect explorations continued. When Barak ousted Netanyahu in elections in 1999, hopes for a quick resumption and conclusion of negotiations were high. Not only did Barak give priority to the Syrian over the Palestinian track, he also stated that all his predecessors since Rabin, including Netanyahu, had been prepared to withdraw to the June 1967 lines. While both countries still had different priorities - Syria's prime interest being the restitution of its occupied territory, Israel's normal relations and reliable security arrangements – an agreement seemed close. In December 1999 and January 2000, US-sponsored high-level talks took place in Washington and Shephardstown in Virginia. They were discontinued after the leak to the Israeli press, which embarrassed the Syrian negotiators, of a US-drafted document which showed Syria's readiness to make substantial concessions over security and normalisation, even though major disagreements regarding the border question persisted. In March, Clinton met Asad in Geneva, and brought him a new territorial proposal from Barak. The meeting ended in failure. Israeli, Syrian and US observers widely agree that, during the Shephardstown talks, Syria was prepared to reach an agreement, but Barak was not. At the Clinton-Asad summit, however, the Syrian president rejected the deal which Clinton offered on Barak's behalf. Whether this was because of Asad's deteriorating health, because he was preoccupied with the preparations for his son's succession or, as Syrians see it, because he was offended by the way in which Clinton tried to make him accept a deal that would not return the north-eastern shore of the Lake Tiberias/Sea of Galilee to Syria, is unclear.

While Israelis and Syrians were convinced that negotiations on their bilateral track would be resumed at some point, this was not expected to happen in the near future. In May, instead of waiting for a deal with Syria, Israel unilaterally withdrew its troops from the Lebanese border zone occupied since 1978. This changed the Israeli-

Syrian strategic situation by removing the raison d'être for the guerrilla war which Hizbollah had led against the Israeli occupation, as well as for Syria's support of that war. Two weeks later, Hafiz al-Asad died. Neither Bashar al-Asad nor Barak saw any urgency in resuming bilateral negotiations.

For Syria's new president and his team, it was clear that Syria had an interest in a peaceful settlement with Israel. However, the reasoning had changed. Hafiz al-Asad's adage that the peace process was Syria's 'strategic option' clearly referred to the regional and international balance of forces. Under Bashar al-Asad, the same motto gained wider meaning. It now pertained mainly to Syria's development chances: Syria needed peace with Israel to pursue its modernisation project.[26] Ironically, these pragmatic insights were not what shaped the international image of Syria's new leadership. Less than three months after Bashar al-Asad's inauguration, bloody confrontations erupted between Israelis and Palestinians, and soft-spoken peace talk moved into the background of Syria's public discourse. Instead, the regime and the president himself reverted to a stark hard-line rhetoric, using vocabulary with regard to Israel unheard of from Arab leaders within the peace process. Asad repeatedly spoke of the Israelis as Nazis and of Israel's efforts to subdue the Palestinian rebellion as a new Holocaust; criticised Arab governments for maintaining relations with Israel; and left no doubt that Syria supported the *intifada*.[27] The US and Israeli media began to portray Bashar al-Asad as a foreign-policy hawk, if not a warmonger.

At the same time, the Syrian leadership made clear that it did not want to be dragged into a confrontation with Israel. Messages to that effect were sent to Israel, mainly through European or US channels, whenever tensions seemed to grow to dangerous levels. Asad repeatedly confirmed Syria's readiness to resume peace talks. Syria, the president explained in a December 2003 interview with *The New York Times*, maintained that negotiations 'should resume from the point at which they had stopped', but did not have any conditions for the resumption of talks.[29] Syria also supported the Saudi Middle East peace initiative adopted at the Beirut Arab Summit of March 2002, and the demand for an 'effective and constructive' American engagement was regularly repeated.

The obvious ambivalence between a realistic interest in leaving the road to eventual peace open and the president's hard-line position has mainly been due to domestic policy considerations. Apparently, Asad did not care over-much whether his rhetoric pleased the US or Europe, let alone Israel.[30] Rather than taking his discourse as proof that he acted under the influence of the 'old guard',[31] however, Asad's rhetoric should be understood as a kind of calculated populism: a conscious attempt to enhance his popularity among the young generation in Syria and other Arab countries, and thereby increase his assets at home. In January 2003, Asad confided to a student delegation that 'Syria derives its position and its directions from the orientation of the Arab street'.[32] Up to and throughout the Iraq war, this approach was largely successful. 'I know', one younger, well-informed and critical Syrian confided to this author, 'that the President's comparisons between Israelis and Nazis etc. do not help us internationally. But given the silence of other Arab leaders in regard to the Palestinian situation, it makes you happy and proud to hear your own president speak up.'

Syria's unresolved conflict with Israel still provides the context for its relations with Lebanon. Since it emerged from civil war in 1991, Lebanon's so-called Second Republic has been under Syrian domination. Syria has supervised Lebanon's foreign policy and strictly controlled security matters and access to the highest political positions. Some among Syria's political and security leaders have exploited Syria's position in Lebanon for illegal gains, and have thereby developed an interest in perpetuating the Syrian presence. For the political leadership, under Hafiz as well as Bashar al-Asad, the rationale for controlling Lebanon has always been linked to the conflict with Israel: in Hafiz al-Asad's understanding of regional power politics, Lebanon could not be neutral as long as that conflict persisted; it would either be under Syrian or Israeli influence. In case of a military confrontation with Israel, Lebanon (particularly the Bekaa valley through which the Beirut–Damascus motorway runs) would be Syria's weak flank.

Israel's unilateral withdrawal from Lebanon in May 2000 not only changed the geopolitics of the Syrian–Israeli conflict, but also raised the political costs of Syria's presence: once the UN had confirmed Israel's withdrawal and demarcated the border, international as well as domestic legitimacy for Hizbollah's military activities ceased. It was widely understood in Lebanon and Syria that ongoing Hizbollah operations against Israeli positions in the Shebaa farms – a 20-square-kilometre piece of land in the Lebanese–Syrian border region[33] – were taking place on behalf of Syria: Damascus wanted to keep a certain level of pressure on Israel, but did not want to implicate its own troops, nor did it want to escalate the confrontation by breaking the ceasefire at the Israeli–Syrian disengagement line in the Golan. Syria's support for Hizbollah and its presence in Lebanon became harder to defend. Moreover, along with and after the Israeli withdrawal, calls for a withdrawal of Syrian troops and a reduction of Syrian influence increased from within Lebanon's civil society and political élite. The Maronite Patriarch demanded the restoration of Lebanon's sovereignty, but unease with the Syrian presence and calls for a 'correction' of the Syrian-Lebanese relationship were not restricted to the Christian community. The Syrian leadership responded to the new situation by reducing its troop presence from some 30,000 to an estimated 20,000 or less, and redeploying most of the remainder from Beirut, the coastal areas and Mount Lebanon to the Bekaa. While Syria's military intelligence maintained its control over Lebanese politics, direct interference in Lebanon's political affairs also decreased. Syrian leaders showed greater leniency with regard to political opposition in Lebanon, and efforts to strengthen the functional cooperation between the two countries were undertaken. The obvious aim was to build a solid basis for strong relations even after a further lessening of Syrian control and an eventual total withdrawal of Syrian troops.[34]

As long as a state of conflict, and the eventuality of war, between Syria and Israel persists, full withdrawal is unlikely. Instead, Syria's leadership will try to maintain the current, pro-Syrian constellation of forces in Lebanon and present itself as a guarantor of Lebanon's stability, and as the only force able to rein in Hizbollah. While the south of Lebanon had largely been under Hizbollah's control after Israel's withdrawal, Syria endorsed the deployment of Lebanese army units to the south prior to the Iraq war,[35] indicating that neither Syria nor Lebanon had any interest in destabilising the situation during the expected US invasion of Iraq. US threats and pressure after the Iraq war were mainly related to Syria's open opposition to the US occupation and to its support for militant Palestinian groups. Lebanon remained an issue, but it was not a priority on the US-Syrian agenda. Thus, when Syria withdrew more troops from Lebanon in mid-2003, the assertion that this was not in any way a response to American pressure[36] was not entirely wrong. On the one hand, the Syrian leadership was largely confident that Lebanon's domestic situation would not cause it any major difficulties in the immediate future: Lebanon's post-civil war institutional setting had proved fairly robust, and the position of pro-Syrian loyalists in the Lebanese government had been strengthened through a cabinet reshuffle in April 2003. Relations between Damascus and Lebanese Christian opposition leaders, including the Maronite Patriarch, had also considerably improved during the Iraq crisis and war, not least because of Syria and the Vatican's similar opposition to the war. A continued reduction of Syria's troop presence would therefore give positive signals without actually risking Syria's influence over strategic matters in Lebanon. Washington, on the other hand, would probably not put too much pressure on Syria over Lebanon. Demands for Syria to leave the country were part of the Syria Accountability Act, but for the US administration it was clear that Syrian troops would remain in Lebanon as long as Hizbollah maintained a guerrilla force; their objective, therefore, was to secure Syrian cooperation in restraining Hizbollah and eventually guaranteeing its disarmament.

Syria has no interest in a military confrontation with Israel, and it will certainly not allow Hizbollah to drag it into military adventures. Syrian officials tend to assume that Israel might seek a pretext for attacking Syria. Given that the US administration would probably not prevent Israel from launching a 'punitive' attack on Syria, they take seriously threats from the Sharon government that Syrian targets would be struck in response to Hizbollah actions. Syria has no absolute control over Hizbollah, nor does Hizbollah seek Syrian permission for each individual operation, though it does coordinate with Damascus, and it would hardly be able to survive as a military force without Syrian support.[37] Consequently, Hizbollah has largely refrained from military operations in the months preceding the Iraq war and since.[38] The quest for a liberation of the Shebaa farms has virtually disappeared from Lebanon's and Hizbollah's political rhetoric, and the latter's military posture is aimed at deterring Israel from launching an attack on the organisation, rather than preparing for aggression against Israel.[39]

At the same time, Syria has an interest in maintaining what local observers call the 'resistance card' as long as Israel occupies

Syrian territory. Demands to disarm Hizbollah or to withdraw it from the border region have therefore been refused. In addition, Asad personally seems to have great respect for Hizbollah leader Hassan Nasrallah, who also enjoys some popularity among Syria's younger generation, not least within the president's own Alawi community. Syria's support for Hizbollah thus has domestic appeal. Under present circumstances, Syria will not move against Hizbollah even under the threat of US sanctions. In the medium term, however, pending continued pressure and some progress in the peace process, Syria may well use its influence to convince Hizbollah to accept disarmament for a stake in the Lebanese government.

This does not imply that the Syrian leadership would ignore the signs of displeasure which it received from the US administration since the end of the Iraq war. At their mildest, US officials describe Syria as not 'responding' sufficiently to US demands for an end to its support for terrorist activities.[40] Other officials have labelled Syria a 'rogue' or a 'dangerous' regime, not least in the debate on sanctioning the country.[41] While Syrian leaders have played down the Syria Accountability Act – Asad has described the Congressional deliberations as a domestic US policy issue[42] – they are aware of the costs of a conflict with the US. Even without new legislation, US pressure and sanctions on Syria have been a nuisance, not least for those in the leadership who have been trying to drive the president's modernisation agenda forward. Syrian officials have complained that US export controls retarded the establishment of the country's internet infrastructure, and that American pressure made Japan, an important supplier of technology, refrain from supporting the modernisation and expansion of Syria's main seaport.[43]

The Syrian leadership has therefore sought an acceptable degree of cooperation with the US in most aspects of regional policy, and is likely to continue to do so. This means in particular not undermining American efforts to stabilise Iraq. The other main post-war US demand on Syria has been to support – or at least not subvert – international efforts to restart the Israeli–Palestinian peace process and, more concretely, to expel the leaders of militant Palestinian organisations such as Hamas and Islamic Jihad. While Syria claims that these organisations, aside from representing parts of the Palestinian refugee population in Syria, were only pursuing press and information activities, their offices were nonetheless closed after the war, and their public activities in Damascus ceased.[44] At the same time, the Syrian leadership was eager not to appear to be caving in to US pressure, and Asad and his ministers and advisors made it clear that Syria would not give up its political support for the *intifada*. As Asad put it: 'No one can give us lessons.'[45]

The Syrian leadership did not endorse the 'roadmap' for peace in the Middle East, but also made clear that it would not seek to undermine it. Syria's main reservation was that the 'map' did not properly address the Syrian and Lebanese tracks. Syria left no doubt that it was interested in a resumption of peace talks with Israel. Asad reportedly sent messages to that effect to Sharon; even though Syria officially denied that such meetings had taken place, he even apparently authorised his younger brother Maher to lead secret talks with Eitan Ben Tsur, a former director of Israel's foreign ministry, in Amman.[46] Members of Syria's political élite are full of misgivings with regard to Israel and its intentions – and not just those of the Sharon government; they often dismiss any differentiation between Israel's 'right' and 'left'.[47] But they also remain convinced that a peaceful solution will eventually be found. 'I might not like the idea,' said a Ba'ath party leadership member, 'but, yes, I think I will see the Israeli flag on an embassy in Damascus.'[48] Peace, then, would also enable speedier modernisation and political reform.

Asad and his team are more likely to develop a positive, cooperative attitude towards any international efforts at resuming the Middle East peace process when US-sponsored Israeli–Syrian negotiations resume, or when a new Madrid-type conference appears in the offing. They are clearly expecting European as well as – and primarily – US support to get the Syrian–Israeli conflicted resolved. Syria's leadership élite is also convinced that the US will need Syria at some point, both in Iraq and in the peace process, and therefore will eventually give greater consideration to Syria's interests.[49] This could, however, be an erroneous assumption, at least with regard to the current US administration. Rather than trying to enlist Syria in a common effort to reinvigorate the peace process, the Bush administration has signalled that Damascus may be dispensable in the post-Iraq war regional environment. In contrast to the EU, Washington did not want to include Syria in the roadmap, let alone have a special roadmap for the Syrian and Lebanese tracks. Syria was excluded from the summit at Sharm al-Sheikh between Bush and a group of Arab leaders in June 2003. There are no signs that, in the near future, Washington will be prepared to back a resumption of bilateral negotiations between Syria and Israel, and thereby help Syria to regain its territory. Instead, the US administration will probably condition its potential engagement with the Syrian (and Lebanese) track on major – but unlikely – changes in Syria's regional policy approach, particularly its support for Palestinian militants. Syria may thus find itself in a prolonged stalemate on the peace process, with all that this implies for the chances of domestic political change.

Conclusion

Domestic Demands and Regional Risks

The Iraq war revived domestic politics in Syria, as well as changing the geopolitical environment. The outcome of the war made Syrians think about their own country's future, and its political system. Shortly after the fall of Baghdad, some 120 leftist and moderate Islamist opposition figures from inside and outside the country published a common statement denouncing American threats against Syria, but also spelling out that 'aggression against Iraq had proved that the security agencies and a one-party [state] are not able to defend the fatherland'. Confronting 'American–Israeli threats and aggression' was impossible 'without a national consensus and a domestic front built on the freedom of the citizens'. Public freedoms should be granted, and a national-unity government formed as the basis for building a 'modern, democratic republic'.[1] In June, a broader group launched a petition calling for 'freedom of opinion, expression, assembly, movement, travel [and] unionist and political activity', and calling on the president to prevent the security agencies from interfering in political life.[2]

Syria's political leadership did not heed such advice, but it had to face a shift of the public mood. Public opinion had largely supported Asad's course before and during the Iraq war. Even dissenters had held back calls for political reform or democracy lest they be seen as part of an American agenda. After the fall of the Ba'thist regime in Baghdad, and despite the differences between the two branches of the Ba'th party and their regimes, individuals even within the regime acknowledged that Syria would also have to prepare for change.

There were different answers to the question of what kind of domestic change would be needed. Reform-oriented technocrats in the government expected the speedier implementation of administrative and economic reform. Some of the younger, mid-level Ba'thist leaders spoke of changing parts of the party leadership, and expected a party law that would allow for more pluralism and more competitive legislative elections. Direct criticism of the president also became louder, nurtured only partly by companions of his late father, with unfavourable comparisons being drawn between the president's apparent miscalculation over the war, and Hafiz al-Asad's dexterity in handling the 1990–91 Gulf crisis.

Under the elder Asad, Syria had developed a significant ability to wait out international pressure and regional crises. The situation following the 2003 Iraq war was, however, different from former crises. Bashar al-Asad has to face a combination of unfavourable regional developments, a much more assertive US leadership, a difficult political-economic inheritance and expectations of domestic reform which he himself created. And, of course, there is the question of experience: following the fall of Baghdad, it was not clear whether the Syrian leadership had fully grasped the depth of the new geopolitical reality and its implications.

Regime Stability

The president's domestic position has not, however, been threatened. Since his accession in July 2000, Bashar al-Asad has built up his authority within the political system in a gradual but calculated manner. He is still seen as the heir to, rather than the builder of, the strong, authoritarian state he presides over, and he still has to prove his strength – otherwise, neither the arrests and trials of dissenters in 2001 nor his hard-line populist posturing towards Israel or during the Iraq war would have been necessary. But Asad can clearly get his way, even against resistance from within the system.[3]

In many ways, the new regime has not liberated itself from the old. A critical, public debate about Hafiz al-Asad and his era has yet to begin. Criticism of government policies in that era has become common currency, but the late president and his foreign- and domestic-policy decisions remain taboo. Although Bashar al-Asad continues to rely on some of his father's key aides, he has been able to rejuvenate the political élite and create a loyal base within the main pillars of the system – the Ba'th party, the administration and the security apparatus – as well as the parliament and the 'popular organisations', such as trade and student unions. Any rebellion against Bashar al-Asad would be likely to threaten the entire regime. This is a strong disincentive against any insurrection by individuals within the regime élite.

Official representatives of Syria are largely right when they stress the stability of the system as such. Regime stability under Hafiz as well as Bashar al-Asad has relied on several factors. The political system itself is based on an institutional arrangement that makes any constitutional change or change of government dependent on the will of the president. Political contenders have practically no space, and there is no credible opposition with wide-ranging popular appeal.[4] Moreover, there is clearly a broad societal quest for stability, which includes a sometimes uneasy, but generally acquiescent, acceptance of a paternalistic and authoritarian state. Many Syrians fear that the demise of the regime could bring back the military coups and counter-coups of the 1950s and 1960s or, worse, the sectarian tensions and bloody confrontations between the regime and radical Islamists in the 1970s and 1980s. The memory of this confrontation has also de-legitimised those brands of the Islamist current that resorted to terrorism and armed insurrection.

Today, confessionalism hardly suffices as an explanation of Syrian politics,[5] even though confessional and regional loyalties continue to stabilise patronage networks. The president is a member of the Alawite branch of Shi'ite Islam, and many positions, particularly in the security apparatus, are controlled by Alawis or by members of Asad's family. However, an increasing number of social, economic and political networks transcend such 'primordial' lines - the Computer Society, business networks and civil-society committees are all cases in point. Even the banned Muslim Brotherhood, which led the anti-regime struggle in the 1980s, has ceased to play on confessional divisions, stressing instead human rights, the rule of law, pluralism and national unity.

Although the predefined results of Syria's parliamentary election cannot be taken as an authentic reflection of popular opinion, the regime and its party do enjoy legitimacy among important segments of the population, particularly the rural lower and middle classes and parts of the salaried middle class. In these strata and others, many are unhappy with the state of the economy, the arrogance of the political class, the lack of accountability or the spread of corruption – but there is a strong feeling within these groups that one owes one's social position to the Ba'thist policies of the 1960s or 1970s.[6] There is also a wide and genuine respect for the nationalistic stance and foreign-policy achievements of Hafiz al-Asad, and for the political stability achieved under his regime.

For decades, rent inflows such as foreign aid or net gains from Iraqi oil deliveries have been important in strengthening the regime's patronage capacity, and thereby maintaining the loyalty of strategic groups. Such inflows have become more precarious, but this does not necessarily translate into an immediate loss of political support or acquiescence. The regime has been able to shield itself against such effects through its economic policies: an economic opening that allows the upper middle class to live a good life and, under Bashar al-Asad, more expansive fiscal policies which have helped to improve living conditions for most state employees.

Fundamentally, the regime retains all the instruments of authoritarianism, and uses them where it deems it necessary. However, repression has become much more selective than it used to be, and is even cloaked in a semblance of rule-of-law and institutional procedure. Syrians are debating politics quite freely, if not always publicly, and they generally experience more openness, particularly to foreign media and to the internet, as well as to commerce and travel. Political life has become more pluralistic. This does not, however, mean that the security apparatus has lost its clout. People fear it less, but the *mukhabarat* is still an essential means of control.

Domestic Development and External Conflict

Bashar al-Asad inherited an economy in dire need of reform. Public finance and the economy still depend on dwindling oil revenues and other unreliable incomes. Much state finance is eaten away by a largely ineffective bureaucracy, the public sector produces deficits, private capital is loath to invest and rising unemployment and increasing income differentials constitute a threat to social stability. New oil finds may be made, and Syria may profit from a reconstruction boom in Iraq – if such a boom comes about. But this is unlikely to put the economy on its feet without a clear shift towards a market economy and a reliable investment climate.

Asad and his technocratic team have made economic and administrative reform their priority. To avoid a Russian-style economic breakdown, they have chosen a gradualist approach.

Nonetheless, an impressive series of new regulations and laws has been introduced, all in some way designed to modernise economic structures and open up space for private entrepreneurship. Differences within the regime élite about the scope and speed of reform have remained, and the implementation of new legislation has been difficult due to bureaucratic resistance, inefficiency and lack of skills. At bottom, the success of economic reform will depend on more than administrative reform; it will also demand that modicum of political reform which economic and societal actors will need to feel reassured and able to engage. This means guaranteeing the rule of law and building an effective justice system, rather than allowing well-connected individuals to stay outside its reach. It will also mean serious steps towards more accountable and transparent governance and, eventually, democratic participation.

Syria's political leadership has sought to widen the scope of representation within the country's political-institutional system, particularly parliament, by co-opting individuals representing strategic parts of the broader societal élite, such as the business community, technocrats and intellectuals. However, it has not permitted political competition. In Asad's agenda, modernisation comes before any democratisation, and the process of 'development and modernisation' has to be led and controlled from the centre. On this basis, a coalition of regime conservatives and modernisers was possible, rather than an alliance of Asad's reform team with the liberal, democratic current that had hoped to see the young president as a vehicle for the system's transformation.

Ironically, in many respects Syria seems 'riper' for a more pluralistic, democratic system than other states in the region: state institutions have widely penetrated society; the state holds a monopoly over the legitimate means of violence; the population is generally well-educated; there is a lively middle class; and opposition forces dismiss violence as an instrument of political change, and would be prepared to support a gradual, consensual transition involving the president and parts of the wider leadership. This leadership, however, has a different agenda: it emphasises technical and economic modernisation, but fails to involve, and thereby discourages, the very people that would be needed for comprehensive reform. Under this premise, even the prospects for economic progress seem doubtful.

Domestic developments are, of course, influenced by external factors. The internal political debate was revivified with the fall of Baghdad. Domestic pressure for change would probably have increased if Iraq's invasion and occupation had been followed by quick and visible progress to a stable and more democratic regime. At earlier stages, progress in the Arab-Israeli peace process strengthened the more economically and politically liberal elements in the Syrian regime, while the breakdown of negotiations and the electoral victories of the Israeli right boosted hardliners.[7] Bashar al-Asad has repeatedly said that Syria needs peace in order to pursue his modernisation programme, and it can reasonably be assumed that little could spur economic growth, investment and political reform in Syria more than a peace accord with Israel.[8] The Syrian regime may seem outdated, but it would be easier to reform it in the absence of a state of confrontation which not only blocks resources, but also frequently closes minds. The repression of dissent in 2001 has been justified by regime loyalists on grounds of regional threats and tensions. Parts of the opposition – particularly nationalists and Islamists – are prepared to put their dissent on hold or even, in the words of one opposition leader, to 'align themselves with the regime', if external, particularly American, pressure on Syria increases.[9]

Syria's environment has become neither friendlier nor easier to handle since the US became, in Foreign Minister Sharaa's words, one of its neighbours.[10] In addition, Israel has been seeking to change the rules of the regional game, a shift clearly demonstrated by an air attack on a disused Palestinian training camp on Syrian territory in early October 2003. The attack – the first of its kind since the 1973 war – was designed to tell Syria that it might not be able to evade a direct, military confrontation if it continued to support Palestinian militants. More worrying for Syria than the attack as such was the fact that it obviously had Washington's consent. Shortly afterwards, the Syria Accountability Act was approved by Congress.

Syrian leaders were concerned by this turn of events, but not overtly alarmed. The general assumption was that the US would not press for domestic political change in Syria, and that Washington would eventually need Syria if it was to secure peace and stability in the Middle East. They seem to be right on the first assumption: regime change on the Iraqi model has not been part of the US agenda, and political reform in Syria is not a US priority in its dealings with

Damascus.[11] As for the second, Syria's leadership underestimated Washington's unhappiness with what the US describes as Syria's lack of cooperation, and overestimated Washington's readiness to help in a resumption of the Syrian–Israeli peace process. The Bush administration will make no effort to restart negotiations as long as Syria is seen to be 'on the wrong side of the war on terror', i.e. as long as it does not change its position on Islamic Jihad and *Hamas*, and more generally on armed resistance to Israeli occupation. However, such a reversal of Syria's stance is not likely, certainly not in the absence of a meaningful peace process.

Washington, for its part, may underestimate the potential volatility of the situation and the lasting importance of an Israeli-Syrian settlement for regional peace and Arab 'normalisation' with Israel.[13] If the US were to give the impression that limited escalation was acceptable and that it had given up on its commitment to broker a Syrian–Israeli peace accord, this would send wrong, and potentially dangerous, signals to both countries. Rather, out of their interest both to stabilise the region and give an impetus for change in Syria and other countries, the US and Europe should continue to seek a fair and comprehensive solution to the Middle East conflict that includes Syria and, by extension, Lebanon.

For bilateral relations with Damascus, a form of conditional engagement may be appropriate: this would involve a clear message that there is room for increased cooperation, including trade, an enhanced political dialogue – as foreseen, on Europe's part, under the EU–Syria Association Agreement – the modernisation of economic and administrative structures, technology and education and cultural and civil-society exchange. There are partners to speak to in Syria. Conditional engagement would imply the linkage of a deepening and intensified political contact and economic cooperation with further political opening and the implementation of a reform agenda which Syrian decision-makers and civil society are perfectly able to design by themselves.

Notes

Introduction

[1] See Patrick Seale, *Asad of Syria: The Struggle for the Middle East* (London: I. B. Tauris, 1988).

[2] Moshe Ma'oz, *Syria and Israel: From War to Peacemaking* (Oxford: Clarendon Press, 1995).

[3] For such an approach see Daniel Pipes, *Greater Syria: The History of an Ambition* (New York: Oxford University Press, 1990).

[4] See, for example, Abu-As'ad Khalil, 'Syria and the Arab-Israeli Conflict', *Current History*, vol. 93, no. 580, February 1994, pp. 83–86.

[5] See, for example, Raymond Hinnebusch and Alasdair Drysdale, *Syria and the Middle East Peace Process* (New York: Council on Foreign Relations, 1991); and Seale, *Asad of Syria*.

[6] See Volker Perthes, 'Si vis stabilitatem, para bellum: State Building, National Security and War Preparation in Syria', in Steven Heydemann (ed.), *War, Institutions, and Social Change in the Middle East* (Berkeley, CA: University of California Press, 2000), pp. 149–73.

Chapter 1

[1] For an account, see Sakina Boukhaima, 'Bachar el-Assad: chronique d'une succession en Syrie', *Monde arabe: Maghreb-Machrek*, no. 169, July–September 2000, pp. 164–72.

[2] For an English version of Asad's inaugural speech, see *Syria Times*, 18 July 2000.

[3] 'Elite' here has a purely functional connotation, referring to those who take, or have influence on, decisions of political relevance. See Volker Perthes, 'Syria: Difficult Inheritance', in Volker Perthes (ed.), *Arab Elites: Negotiating the Politics of Change* (Boulder, CO: Lynne Rienner, forthcoming 2004).

[4] ArabNews.com, 18 January 2003.

[5] Al-Arabiyah Television (Dubai), 9 June 2003.

[6] Private communication, Damascus, June 2003.

[7] Alan George, Syria: *Neither Bread nor Freedom* (London and New York: Zed Books, 2003).

[8] On the cult and its function, see Lisa Wedeen, *Ambiguities of Domination: Politics, Rhetoric, and Symbols in Contemporary Syria* (Chicago, IL: University of Chicago Press, 1999).

[9] Among the many books that stress the patrimonial aspects of the Asad regime, see in particular Nikolaos van Dam, *The Struggle for Power in Syria: Politics and Society under Asad and the Ba'th Party* (London: I. B. Tauris, 1996).

10 On the structures of authoritarianism, see Volker Perthes, *The Political Economy of Syria under Asad* (London: I. B. Tauris, 1995), pp. 133–202.

11 *Syria Times*, 18 July 2000.

12 For an English version of the 'Statement [or Memorandum] of the 99', see George, *Syria*, pp. 178ff.

13 Ibid., p. 42.

14 For a more detailed narrative of events, see ibid., pp. 30–46; and Phillipe Droz-Vincent, 'Syrie: la nouvelle generation au pouvoir', *Monde arabe: Maghreb-Machrek*, no. 173, 2001, pp. 14–38.

15 For an English translation, see George, *Syria*, pp. 182–88.

16 Khaddam's speech of 18 February 2001 is documented in *al-Hayat*, 10 July 2001.

17 *al-Sharq al-Awsat*, 8 February 2001.

18 *al-Hayat*, 15 April 2001.

19 Interview, *al-Majalla*, no. 1,108, 6–12 May 2001. Tlass continued: 'We came up with various military moves, and we paid with our blood for the power'.

20 See *al-muharrir al-'arabi*, 24–30 March 2001; *al-Doumari*, 23 April 2001.

21 *al-Thaura*, 3 March 2001, quoted in BBC Summary of World Broadcasts, 6 March 2001.

22 Published in *al-Hayat*, 16 April 2001.

23 See *Middle East International*, 17 May 2002; *al-Hayat*, 1 August 2002. Turk was released on a special presidential pardon in November 2002, ironically on the anniversary of the former president's assumption of power.

24 Interviews, Damascus, June 2003.

25 Interviews, Damascus, June 2003.

26 The quote is from Asad's interview with *al-Sharq al-Awsat*, 8 February 2001; the theme is recurrent in his speeches and interviews.

27 See Volker Perthes, 'Syria's Parliamentary Elections: Remodeling Asad's Political Base', *Middle East Report*, vol. 22, no. 1, 1992.

28 The SSNP, founded by the Lebanese Antoun Saadeh in Beirut in 1932, is a secular, nationalist party committed to the idea of 'Greater Syria'. Historically a fierce rival of the Ba'th and the idea of Arab nationalism, its two main wings have moved closer to the Syrian regime, particularly since the Israeli invasion of Lebanon in 1982 and the participation of the SSNP in resistance activities.

29 See Asad's inaugural speech and the *al-Sharq al-Awsat* interview of 8 February 2001.

30 The latest conference of the Arab Socialist Union, for example, was held under the slogan 'Towards a renewed Nasserist party that deepens its belonging to the school of the eternal leader Hafiz al-Asad and stands firmly in line behind the leadership of President Bashar al-Asad' (*Akhbar al-Sharq*, 27 July 2003).

31 See the Syrian Muslim Brotherhood's so-called 'Project for a national charter of honour', published in *al-Hayat*, 4 May 2001.

32 Bahjat Sulaiman, 'Suriya wa-l-tahdidat al-amrikiyya' [Syria and the American threats], *al-Safir*, 15 May 2003. General Sulaiman is the head of the domestic branch of General Intelligence.

33 Differences between these accounts remain huge. While well-informed observers (in personal conversations with the author) put the figure at less than 20%, the minister of the interior gave a figure of 63.4%, acknowledging a decrease of almost 20 percentage points in comparison to the 1999 elections (*Neue Zürcher Zeitung*, 7 March 2003).

34 See Perthes, *The Political Economy of Syria*, pp. 154–61.

35 Syria's confusing way of dealing with the UN Security Council decision on Resolution 1483 pro-

vides an example. The majority in the party leadership, including the foreign minister, were clearly opposed to a resolution that would legitimise, in one way or other, a US-led occupation of Iraq, and the Syrian ambassador at the UN stayed away from the vote. Asad, who was unhappy with this behaviour, which did not help to improve the country's international image, directed the foreign minister to inform the party leadership that the president wanted its consent to a Syrian acceptance of the resolution; he received it without even attending the leadership meeting. The next day, Syria informed the Security Council that its vote should be registered as 'Yes' (Personal conversations, Damascus, June 2003).

[36] Press statement issued by the Civil Society Committees, quoted in *Akhbar al-Sharq*, 29 July 2003.

[37] Asad was frank about this in an interview with Austria's *Der Standard*: 'A development process should take place on an overall basis, it should be economic, social and political in every field. But one area undoubtedly comes first and just which one depends on where it will be easier and hence faster' (quoted in *BBC Summary of World Broadcasts*, 1 April 2003).

Chapter 2

[1] UNDP, Human Development Report 2003.

[2] For statistical date in this chapter, unless otherwise indicated see *Syrian Statistical Abstract 2002*. Much of Syria's statistics should be treated with great caution; often, statistical figures show development trends rather than true numbers.

[3] On the development of Syria's economy and economic policies see Perthes, *The Political Economy of Syria*; Nabil Sukkar, *al-islah al-*

iqtisadi fi suriya [Economic Reform in Syria] (Beirut: Riad El-Rayyes Books, 2000).

[4] According to Syria's prime minister, the growth rate in 2002 was 3.3%, slightly above population growth. See his interview with the Oxford Business Group, distributed electronically 11 April 2003.

[5] The estimate is conservative because it assumes that, on average, less than 55% of the relevant age group actually try to find a job; it does not consider any significant increase of economic activity through, mainly, an increase in female participation in the labour force. All figures in this paragraph, unless otherwise indicated, are based on the *Syrian Statistical Abstract 2002*.

[6] It is widely accepted that official unemployment figures – over the years set at 9–10% – understated the problem. Significantly, the *2002 Statistical Abstract* no longer provides any figures on this.

[7] See, among others, 'Izz al-Din Juni, *al-tijara al-kharijiyya al-suriyya khilal rub' al-qarn al-madi* [Syrian Foreign Trade in the Last Quarter Century] (Damascus: Dar al-Rida li-l-nashr, 2002), pp. 310–24; for an overview of Syria's oil sector, see the US Energy Intelligence Agency's country analysis brief 'Syria', www.eia.doe.gov/emeu/cabs/syria.html.

[8] *al-Hayat*, 1 July 2002.

[9] According to then Minister of Industry Isam al-Zaim, the accumulated losses of the public industrial sector reached $1.6 billion in 2001 (*The Syria Report*, 10 January 2002), i.e. around one quarter of that year's budget.

[10] For a recent Syrian account, see Husein al-Qadi, *al-islah al-iqtisadi fi suriya ila ayn?* [Economic Reform in Syria Whereto?] (Damascus: Dar al-Rida li-l-nashr, 2002), pp. 173ff.

[11] *Statistical Abstract*, various years.

[12] Interview with Prime Minister Mustapha Miro, Oxford Business Group, 11 April 2003.

[13] *Statistical Abstract*, various years.

[14] Samir Seifan, 'Perspectives de l'Économie', *Confluences Meditérranéenes*, no. 44, Winter 2002–03. In 2001, according to the Inter-Arab Investment Guarantee Corporation, Arab investments in Syria totalled $43.5 million, while Syrian investments in Arab countries amounted to $305m. *The Syria Report*, 30 May 2002.

[15] Bashar al-Asad, interview with *Der Standard*, 1 April 2003.

[16] No reliable data are available on this issue. It may be realistic to assume that 50% of those employed in the public sector and public administration are relatively poor; they would certainly not be able to make their living from their salary alone, but have to rely on family members, income from second jobs or other, partly illegal, sources. According to unpublished government estimates, 65–70% of those employed by the state actually rely on a second income. Syrian studies based on data from 1995 show that people employed in the private or informal sector are somewhat better off. Taken together, this still means that some 45% of the economically active population have to be considered relatively poor. See Nabil Marzuq, 'al-batala wa-l-faqr fi suriya' [Unemployment and Poverty in Syria], paper presented to the Economic Tuesday Forum, 5 June 2001.

[17] *al-Sharq al-Awsat*, 18 June 2003, quoting a source from Syria's Central Bureau of Statistics. According to Marzuq ('al-batala wa-l-faqr'), about 60% of pupils at primary and intermediate level leave school before graduating.

[18] Inaugural speech, *Syria Times*, 18 July 2000.

[19] Interviews, Damascus, April and June 2003.

[20] Among Arab countries, only Sudan, Yemen and Iraq had a lower connectivity rate. *Middle East Economic Digest*, 27 June 2003.

[21] *The Syria Report*, 4 March 2002; Ibrahim Hamidi, 'A Digital Revolution: "Syria Enters the Information Age"', *The Daily Star*, 13 July 2002.

[22] 'tatbiqan li-shi'ar "al-ma'lumatiyya laysat li-l-jami"' [Implementing the Slogan "IT Is Not for Everybody"], *al-Iqtisadiyya*, 15 June 2003.

[23] Syria's 2003 budget amounted to LS420bn, compared to only LS265bn in 2000.

[24] The Council lowered interest rates for bank loans from an average 9% to 7.5%; further reductions were envisaged.

[25] The process, which started with the Barcelona Conference of 1995, primarily aims at establishing a Euro-Mediterranean free-trade zone and enhancing common security in the Mediterranean. Its membership, aside from the EU states, comprises Algeria, Cyprus, Egypt, Israel, Jordan, Lebanon, Malta, Morocco, the Palestinian Authority, Syria, Tunisia and Turkey. By 2003, all these countries but Syria had signed such association agreements with the EU.

[26] 59% of the respondents expected positive, 9% negative, effects. See Center for Strategic Studies, 'Economic Integration in the Arab Mashreq Countries', Analytical Report, Amman, 2001, www.css-jordan.org. There are no comparable data from earlier or later periods.

[27] Muhammad al-Atrash, 'hawl al-tawahhud al-iqtisadi al-'arabi wa-l-sharaka al-urubiyya' [On Arab Economic Unification and the European Partnership], *al-Mustaqbal al-'arabi*, vol. 24, October 2000, pp. 87–90. Atrash can be described as an economic nationalist. Thus, in a discussion in parliament, he also insisted

that if a stock market was to be established, foreigners should not be allowed to buy into it (see *Tishreen*, 17 May 2003).

[28] For an overview and a contribution to this debate see Ayman Abdel Nour, 'Syrian Views of an Association Agreement with the European Union', *EuroMeSCo Papers* 14, December 2001.

[29] Interview with Industry Minister Za'im, *al-Hayat*, 1 September 2002.

[30] Author's interviews. See also ibid.; *Abyad wa-aswad*, 23 June 2003.

[31] Industry Minister Za'im, quoted in *al-Hayat*, 19 November 2001.

[32] This is not to say that market economies would not allow for corruption. Privatisation certainly does, as has been proved in many Eastern European countries. But a huge public sector whose accounts lack transparency and whose losses are automatically borne by the state is certainly highly conducive to the illegal private appropriation of public funds. This was highlighted by the corruption cases that were publicised in the context of an anti-corruption campaign that Bashar al-Asad started even before he assumed office. Sums were spectacular. In December 2001, one former deputy prime minister and one former transport minister along with a third person were sentenced to jail sentences and ordered to pay back $276m, plus interest, to Syrian Air for fraud in aircraft acquisitions.

[33] Thus, in an interview with Kuwait's *al-Anba'*, also broadcast over Syrian radio, Asad remarked: 'We have expedited the laws, but the problem lies in implementation ... The Syrian citizen wonders why new laws are being made when previous ones have not yet been implemented' (*BBC Monitoring Global Newsline*, 25 May 2003).

[34] Interviews, Damascus, June 2003.

[35] For details, see www.amcham.org.eg/Publications/Business Monthly, July 2002 and January 2003.

[36] See Perthes, 'Kriegsdividende und Friedensrisiken: Überlegungen zu Rente und Politik in Syrien', Orient, vol. 35, no. 3, 1994, pp. 413–24.

[37] Indirectly, Syrian official sources confirmed this figure by their announcement, shortly after the closure of the pipeline by US forces, that Syria would reduce its oil exports for the current year by approximately 150,000 barrels per day. *al-Hayat*, 9 April 2003.

[38] Interviews, Damascus, April and June 2003.

[39] The latest available Syrian Statistical Abstract (2002) does not give any figures for exports to Iraq in 2001. Press reports spoke of an annual bilateral trade exchange of up to $5bn 'and more', which is certainly a large exaggeration (*al-Hayat*, 13 June 2003).

[40] Syria's LS420bn budget for 2003 equals approximately $8bn.

Chapter 3

[1] Some of Syria's regional policy moves and stances helped to create considerable rent income, mainly from Gulf Arab states. For the 1970s and 1980s, one can speak of a veritable war dividend, i.e. of financial aid which Syria received because of, and only because of, its front-line position in the Arab–Israeli conflict. However, it would be a mistake to conclude that Syria's regional policies were driven by the pursuit of rents or other economic gains. Rather, economic interest was subordinated to political objectives and regional politics. Examples include the closure of the Syrian–Iraqi border and the Iraqi pipeline from 1980 until the

late 1990s, and recurrent interference with Jordanian–Syrian trade exchanges in the late 1990s as a means of demonstrating Syria's resentment of Jordan's 'normalisation' with Israel.

2   According to Hafiz al-Asad's perception of Syria's role, the task of creating a balance so as to prevent Israel's domination of the region lies mainly on Syrian shoulders. Syria would coordinate with other, and stronger, Arab players, notably Egypt and Saudi Arabia. While Lebanon's post-civil war governments have all toed the Damascus line, the Palestinians and the Jordanians did not. This explains the deep and seemingly unbridgeable rift between Arafat's and Hafiz al-Asad's regimes, and recurrent conflicts between Syria and Jordan.

3   According to the *IISS Military Balance 2003/4*, Syria's armed forces total 314,000 active soldiers; the number of combat aircraft is 548, the number of main battle tanks 4,500. Note that among the tanks, more than half are T-55s or T-62s, i.e. models from the 1950s and 1970s (figures for Israel, in comparison: total active armed forces 167,600; combat aircraft 438; main battle tanks 3,950). See also, with somewhat higher figures both for Syria and Israel, Shai Feldman and Yiftah Shapir (eds), *The Middle East Military Balance 2000–01* (Tel Aviv and Cambridge, MA: Jaffee Center for Strategic Studies/MIT Press, 2001).

4   Following the Iraq war, some Syrian officials claimed that the country did not possess any weapons of mass destruction (WMD). This may be correct if one does not count chemical arms as WMD. But it was confusing as Syria, at the same time, demanded that the UN deal with all WMD in the region, including, it might be assumed, those in Syrian possession. Syria has not signed the Chemical Weapons Convention, explaining its refusal to do so via Israel's refusal to sign the Nuclear Non-Proliferation Treaty (NPT). See also Bahsar al-Asad's interview with *The Daily Telegraph*, 6 January 2004, where he emphasised that it is 'natural for us to look for means to defend ourselves'. There are also unconfirmed reports of a biological-weapons programme. However, suggestions that Syria has a nuclear-arms programme seem to be politically motivated exaggerations. For assessments of Syrian WMD capability, see Feldman and Shapir (eds), *Middle East Military Balance*, p. 291; *Jane's Foreign Report*, 31 July 2003.

5   *BBC Summary of World Broadcasts*, 15 November 2000.

6   See the speech by Romano Prodi, 17 May 2003, *Euromed Report*, 22 May 2003.

7   See Abdel Nour, 'Syrian Views'.

8   Consequently, Syrian media highlighted British statements to the effect that one would not support US action against Syria, and downplayed Britain's (but not the US) role as an occupying power in Iraq.

9   For trade data, see the annual IMF *Directory of Trade Statistics*. If illicit trade with Iraq and Lebanon were counted, figures would be considerably higher.

10   See Robert Olson, 'Turkey-Syria Relations, 1997 to 2000: Kurds, Water, Israel and "Undeclared War"', *Orient*, vol. 42, no. 1, 2001, pp. 101–17.

11   See Alain Gresh, 'Turkish-Israeli-Syrian Relations and Their Impact on the Middle East', *Middle East Journal*, vol. 52, no. 2, Spring 1998, pp. 188–03.

12   Kurds are estimated to constitute some 10% of the Syrian population, and Kurdish nationalism is less assertive in Syria than in Turkey or Iraq. Still, the Syrian

government has failed, so far, to abolish discriminatory regulations against parts of its Kurdish citizenry that are a source of recurrent tension. The emergence of an independent Kurdish state would arouse fears of possible separatist spill-overs into Syria.

[13] See Anoushiravan Ehteshami and Raymond A. Hinnebush, *Syria and Iran: Middle Powers in a Penetrated Regional System* (London and New York: Routledge, 1997).

[14] See Volker Perthes, *Vom Krieg zur Konkurrenz. Regionale Politik und die Suche nach einer neuen arabisch-nahöstlichen Ordnung* (Baden-Baden: Nomos, 2000), pp. 111–30.

[15] See Asad's speech at the Beirut Arab summit in *al-Hayat*, 28 March 2002.

[16] See Seymour M. Hersh, 'The Syrian Bet', *The New Yorker*, 28 July 2003.

[17] In the weeks preceding the war, Iraq exported large quantities of wheat to Syria, thereby breaking international sanctions which banned all exports from Iraq except for oil exports under international supervision. The benefit was mutual: while selling off its wheat at a substantial discount, the Iraqi regime gained freely disposable cash; Syrian importers profited from the discount. With regard to US accusations that the trucks had brought Iraqi weapons to Syria, Syria's leadership found itself in a dilemma. Had it disclosed the nature of the suspicious truck movements - which given their quantity and illegal nature could not have taken place without the consent and protection of high regime officials – it would also have disclosed its active breach of the Iraq sanctions regime.

[18] See for example Asad's interview in *al-Safir*, 27 March 2003.

[19] The Act calls for US sanctions on Syria unless it halts 'support for terrorism', ends its 'occupation of Lebanon' and stops the development of WMD. Which sanctions will be applied is left to the discretion of the US president; the choice of possible sanctions ranges from a ban on Syrian aircraft landing in the US and travel restrictions for Syrian diplomats to a total ban on US exports to Syria (except for food and medicines) and US investment in Syria. Similar legislation had been proposed in 2002, but was blocked due to objections from the White House.

[20] Several Iraqi officials who had found their way to Syria were sent back and indirectly handed over to US forces; likewise, the wife and daughters of Saddam Hussein, who had sought refuge in Syria before the war, were expelled.

[21] Bassam Hashim, 'al-qawmiyya al-'arabiyya hadaf idiulujiya al-muhafizin al-judud' [Arab Nationalism Is the Aim of the Ideology of the Neo-Conservatives], *al-Ba'th*, 24 April 2003.

[22] See *al-Hayat*, 26 September 2003.

[23] See Oxford Business Group, *Online Briefing Syria*, 6 June 2003.

[24] For preliminary accounts of the Israeli-Syrian bilaterals, see Helena Cobban, *The Israeli-Syrian Peace Talks: 1991–96 and Beyond* (Washington DC: United States Institute for Peace Press, 1999); Eyal Zisser, 'The Israel-Syria Negotiations – What Went Wrong', Orient, vol. 42, no. 1, 2001, pp. 225-51; see also the earlier accounts of the main negotiators in the 1992–96 phase: Itamar Rabinovich, *The Brink of Peace: The Israeli-Syrian Negotiations* (Princeton, NJ: Princeton University Press, 1998); and Walid al-Mu'allim, 'Fresh Light on the Syrian–Israeli Peace Negotiations', *Journal of Palestine Studies*, vol. 26, no. 2/102, Winter 1997, pp. 81–94.

[25] As the line was never demarcated, the concept of 'full withdrawal', or withdrawal to the lines of 1967, is vague and leaves room for intended ambiguity, as well as for compromise. For details on the border and ceasefire lines between Syria and Israel, see Frederic C. Hof, 'The Line of June 4, 1967', *Middle East Insight*, vol. 14, no. 5, September-October 1999, pp. 17–23.

[26] Explicitly: 'Nous devons travailler à la paix pour faire avancer le processus de modernisation', Bashar al-Asad, interview with *Le Figaro*, 23 June 2001.

[27] See, for example, Asad's speech at the Beirut Arab summit in *al-Hayat*, 28 March 2002.

[28] See, for example, 'Syrian President Relays Message to Israeli PM via British Envoy', *Jerusalem Post*, 22 December 2002.

[29] *The New York Times* and www.nytimes.com, 1 December 2003. In contrast to earlier interviews (*Le Figaro*, 23 June 2001), Asad no longer insisted that Israel's government accept the basic principle of the 'Rabin deposit'.

[30] See Anders Strindberg, 'Growth with Strength: Syria's Hardline Reformer', *Jane's Intelligence Review*, vol. 13, no. 2, February 2001, pp. 30–33.

[31] See Eyal Zisser, 'Bashar of Arabia', *Wall Street Journal*, 5 September 2003, p. 8.

[32] Quoted in *al-Hayat*, 12 January 2003.

[33] On the political geography of the region see Frederick C. Hof, 'A Practical Line', *Middle East Journal*, vol. 55, no. 1, Winter 2001, pp. 25–42. There is a dispute about whether the 'farms' are Lebanese territory, as Syria and Lebanon claim in order to prove that Israel's 2000 withdrawal from Lebanon is incomplete, and ongoing resistance thus legitimate, or Syrian (the UN position).

What is undisputed is that they have been under Israeli occupation since 1967.

[34] On Syria's recent policies in Lebanon, see Eric V. Thompson, 'Will Syria Have To Withdraw from Lebanon?', *Middle East Journal*, vol. 56, no. 1, Winter 2002.

[35] *Naharnet*, 10 February 2003.

[36] See statement by Butheina Shaaban, quoted in *al-Hayat*, 23 July 2003.

[37] For a recent evaluation of Hizbollah's capabilities and strategies, see International Crisis Group, 'Hizbullah: Rebel Without a Cause?', *ICG Middle East Briefing*, 30 July 2003.

[38] In August 2003, an exchange of cross-border shelling between Hizbollah and Israeli forces, as well as Israeli overflights of Lebanon - even, reportedly, over the presidential palace in Syria's coastal city Lattakia - could easily have escalated. The crisis was apparently contained by US and Syrian efforts to restrain their allies. For details see *Jane's Defence Weekly*, 20 August 2003.

[39] International Crisis Group, 'Hizbollah', pp. 7–9.

[40] See the remarks of US Secretary of State Colin Powell together with the Kuwait Foreign Minister Sheikh Al-Sabah, 15 September 2003, www.state.gov/secretary/rm/2003.

[41] John Bolton, quoted in *The Financial Times*, 18 September 2003.

[42] See Asad's Interview with *al-Hayat*, 7 October 2003.

[43] Personal communication, Damascus, June 2003. See also the interview with Communication Minister Muhammad Bashir Munajjid in *al-Hayat*, 5 September 2003.

[44] Individual leaders of Hamas or Islamic Jihad maintained residences in Syria and travelled between Syria and other Arab countries, such as Qatar, often on

US passports. See Anders Strindberg, 'Syria's Palestinians Under Fire', *Middle East International*, 22 August 2003. The US administration maintains that the closing down of offices was merely 'cosmetic' – and that the Syrian authorities did not prevent Islamic Jihad or Hamas leaders from planning or directing operations from Damascus. Personal communication, Washington DC, October 2003.

45 Asad's speech to the People's Assembly, 10 March 2003, quoted in *Tishreen*, 11 March 2003.

46 See *al-Hayat*, 6 May, 7 May, 8 May 2003.

47 The Arabs still insisted that in Israel there was a split between the right and the left, Asad said in his speech to the People's Assembly on 10 March 2003. Daily events, however, and Israel's elections proved 'that all of Israel is of the right [wing]'.

48 Personal communication, June 2003.

49 See Patrick Seale, 'Syria and Europe: A Big Step Forward', 26 September 2003, www.mafhoum.com/press6/seal e162.htm.

Conclusion

1 Quoted in *al-Hayat*, 23 April 2003.

2 The petition, with a list of its 287 signatories, was published in the Lebanese daily *al-Safir*, 3 June 2003.

3 The most notable change in the cabinet reshuffle of September 2003, aside from the replacement of Prime Minister Miro with the more respected Muhammad Naji al-Otri, was the replacement of two ministers who had been critical of the prospects of EU association.

4 Riad al-Turk, the veteran communist opposition leader, admitted as much in an interview with Lebanon's *al-Nahar* (29 September 2003), stating that Syria's political opposition was unable to 'achieve tasks of change'.

5 See for more detail Perthes, *Syria under Asad*, pp. 181–87.

6 See Hanna Batatu, *Syria's Peasantry: The Descendants of Its Lesser Rural Notables and Their Politics* (Princeton, NJ: Princeton University Press, 1999).

7 See Volker Perthes, 'Syrie: Le plus gros pari d'Assad', *Politique internationale*, vol. 87 Spring 2000, pp. 177–92.

8 See George, *Syria*, p. 174.

9 See Riad al-Turk's interview, *al-Nahar*, 29 September 2003.

10 Quoted in *International Herald Tribune*, 17 September 2003.

11 Personal communication with senior US officials, June and October 2003.

12 In his interview with *al-Hayat* of 7 October 2003, Asad clearly stated his refusal to expel the exiled leaders of Hamas and Palestinian Jihad: they are not terrorists, he explained, and had not violated any Syrian laws, nor had they harmed Syrian interests.

13 See International Crisis Group, 'Middle East Endgame III: Israel, Syria and Lebanon – How a Comprehensive Peace Settlement Would Look', *ICG Middle East Report*, no. 4, 16 July 2002.